Part One

Blocked

LEADERSHIP

UN BLOCKED

Break Through

the Beliefs

That Limit Your Potential

MURIEL M. WILKINS

HARVARD BUSINESS REVIEW PRESS   BOSTON, MASSACHUSETTS

Copyright 2025 Muriel Maignan Wilkins

Printed in the United States of America

10 9 8 7 6 5 4 3 2 1

The web addresses referenced in this book were live and correct at the time of the book's publication but may be subject to change.

Library of Congress Cataloging-in-Publication data is forthcoming.

ISBN: 978-1-64782-726-7
eISBN: 978-1-64782-727-4

The paper used in this publication meets the requirements of the American National Standard for Permanence of Paper for Publications and Documents in Libraries and Archives Z39.48-1992.

To Maman and Papa—my beginning.
To Arden—my beacon.
To Noah and Gabi—my becoming.
This is for you.

Contents

Part One
BLOCKED

Introduction: We All Get Blocked   3

  1 What's Really Blocking You?   13

  2 How to Get Out of Your Own Way   25

Part Two
THE HIDDEN BLOCKERS

  3 I Need to Be Involved   39

  4 I Need It Done Now   59

  5 I Know I'm Right   83

  6 I Can't Make a Mistake   107

  7 If I Can Do It, So Can You   135

  8 I Can't Say No   161

  9 I Don't Belong Here   183

Part Three
UNBLOCKED

  10 Helping Others Overcome Their Hidden Blockers   207

Conclusion: The Road Ahead   223

Appendix: Coach Yourself Worksheet   227

Notes   231

Index   237

Acknowledgments   243

About the Author   247

"A practical resource to help leaders get out of their own way. If you've ever felt like your worst enemy is you, Muriel Wilkins has guidance to help you become a better boss."

—ADAM GRANT, #1 *New York Times* bestselling author, *Think Again* and *Hidden Potential*; podcast host, *Re:Thinking*

"Turns out the biggest challenge to our success at work is often ourselves. This book gets to the heart of the ways we trip ourselves up and offers practical ways to get us untangled."

—MICHAEL BUNGAY STANIER, author, *The Coaching Habit*

"Muriel Wilkins voices the unspoken doubts even the most accomplished leaders carry. *Leadership Unblocked* is an honest, empowering guide that reminds us that our greatest growth often lies on the other side of self-awareness. A must-read for any leader ready to move from good to great."

—MICHELLE RILEY-BROWN, CEO, Children's National Hospital

"*Leadership Unblocked* is a master class in self-awareness. Muriel Wilkins guides us through the invisible assumptions that quietly shape our leadership—and shows us how to release them so we can lead with more clarity, ease, and impact. This book is the coach every ambitious professional needs."

—DORIE CLARK, executive education faculty, Columbia Business School; *Wall Street Journal* bestselling author, *The Long Game*

"The real power of Muriel Wilkins's *Leadership Unblocked* lies in its specificity: rather than recommending a 'cure-all' approach to effective leadership, her work focuses on specific problems that different types of leaders must overcome. The result is actionable insight for each individual over broad assertions of dubious individual relevance."

—TOM MONAHAN, CEO, Heidrick & Struggles

"A refreshing read! Full of real-life examples and grounded in research, this book invites you to self-reflect, recognize what may be holding you back, and act accordingly. As stated in the book, difficulties are unavoidable, but we can and should control how we deal with them. *Leadership Unblocked* offers a roadmap of how to do it with poise, structure, and confidence. All leaders who want to deliver high impact need to read this book!"

—MAGDALENA NOWICKA MOOK, CEO, International
Coaching Federation

"*Leadership Unblocked* is a powerful guide to getting out of your own way. With wisdom, warmth, and hard-won insight, Muriel Wilkins invites us to confront the hidden beliefs that hold us back—and shows us how to replace them with mindsets that unlock performance, potential, and peace of mind. She delivers the clarity and coaching every leader needs—right when they need it most."

—FRANCES FREI, professor, Harvard Business School;
coauthor, *Unleashed*

Introduction

We All Get Blocked

Focused on the shadow, with my back turned to the light
Too intelligent to see it was me in the way

—LAURYN HILL

Years ago, I took a new job heading a flailing division at an established company. My boss gave me eighteen months to turn things around and make the underperforming unit profitable. "I've got this!" I told myself, and I believed it. And why wouldn't I? My whole life had been about achieving good grades, the best schools, coveted jobs, stellar performance reviews, the fast track to leadership. And now this—a new executive role where the business needed fixing and it was up to me to make it happen. It was a dream come true for a high achiever like me.

Little did I know what lay ahead. The challenge that seemed exciting and energizing in those first few weeks turned into months of pain and frustration. While I was responsible for my group's P&L, much of the work that supported my division's growth plan relied on others in the company—IT, product development, sales, fulfillment, finance. And they didn't want to play the part I had cast them in. In meeting after meeting, I faced resistance. I created a plan; they didn't agree. I established deadlines; they didn't meet them. I gave direction; they didn't follow through. Before I knew it, I was inviting myself to every meeting, asking to be copied on every communication, and bypassing the people I saw as impediments to progress. In my mind I was doing everything right to get the results the company needed; in fact, I was going above and beyond by picking up the slack when others didn't deliver.

I grew more and more frustrated with my colleagues until one day, after a contentious disagreement (OK, it was actually a yelling match) with another executive I was convinced was out to sabotage me, I shut my office door, broke down, and cried. I had hit a wall. No matter how hard I worked and what I did, I couldn't move things along. My coworkers were the only thing between me and my goal to make this business successful. Or so I thought.

I went home that evening, plopped down on the couch next to my life partner, Arden, and sighed dramatically.

"What's wrong?" he asked.

I started in on my usual rant, which by then poor Arden probably knew by heart. "I don't understand the people I work with!" I said. "Why can't they just do what they're supposed to do? If I'm doing my part, why can't they do theirs? It's like no one cares but me. Enough already! I just want to get results and all they want to do is talk, talk, talk. I've just about had it!"

Instead of giving his regular pep talk, however, Arden looked at me and, in the calmest voice, asked, "Did you ever think maybe the problem is you and not them?"

While I'd love to say that the light bulb turned on, my frustration lifted, and I accepted the ownership Arden was suggesting, none of that happened. Nope. Not one bit.

"*What?*" I said. "How could you say that? Clearly you don't know what you're talking about!"

I went to bed even more discouraged than before.

Fast-forward a year, and despite the difficulties, I had managed to turn the division around in record time. My boss rewarded me by adding an even larger division to my plate that needed significant change. While I was pleased with the increased leadership scope, I did not look forward to working with my peers through this even bigger business challenge.

I fell back on the tactics that got me the results with the first division—even though they'd also caused me (and others) a lot of angst. I continued to try to get my colleagues to change. The more I pushed, the more they resisted. The more they resisted, the more I pushed. I was once again caught in a loop, but this time I couldn't see my way out. One day, after a marathon of back-to-back meetings that did nothing but frustrate me, I sat in my office looking out the window and realized I couldn't take it anymore. The struggle was just too much. Exhausted, demoralized, and resentful, I turned in my resignation a few weeks later.

Some time passed before Arden's words came back to me: *Did you ever think the problem is you and not them?* Finally, away from the turmoil work had become, I got it. I'd been so focused on others being the source of my frustrations that I'd ignored the role I'd played in the drama. In my relentless pursuit of the win, I'd failed to realize I couldn't do it all on my own. I was so convinced I knew what needed to be done that I didn't listen to those around me.

I had to face reality: it was easy and comfortable to blame everyone else, but I was part of the problem. A big part. I'd made things much harder on myself and my colleagues than they needed to be, so much so that I ended up quitting.

There had to be a better way. I'd tried everything, but I was blocked and I didn't know why. This moment of clarity ignited questions within me: How could I have gotten through this experience differently, in a way that would have been far less frustrating for my colleagues and for me? Was it possible to navigate my most difficult challenges as a leader with greater ease? I believed it was, but then why had I felt so stuck and unable to see my way out of this?

The quest for answers eventually led me to a career in executive coaching, and over the past two decades, I've found many of the answers I was looking for. I learned I wasn't alone in my struggles as a leader, not even close. *Every* leader gets blocked, even the leadership experts and the leaders who've achieved such extraordinary success they've become household names.

I also realized the truth found in a quote whose origins are unclear but is widely used in Buddhist and personal development circles: "Pain is inevitable. Suffering is optional." In other words, life—and leadership—will never be without their challenging moments. But we have a choice in the way we respond to those moments, and our response can intensify the initial pain and keep us stuck and unproductive—or it can help us navigate those moments with greater ease and position us for future growth. This idea has transformed my approach to leadership, my personal life, and my work with clients. I learned that while many of the sources of our pain are external and out of our control—we get laid off, a colleague betrays our trust, the dream job doesn't come through—much of our subsequent suffering comes from within. When our response is to be overly attached to the way we think things ought to be, resistant to change, or unwilling to let things go, we experience more difficulties and less ease in the way we lead. This is not to blame ourselves for our suffering, but rather to acknowledge that we have a choice in how we respond and don't have to get stuck in a response that increases our distress and impedes our progress.

The realization that there was always a choice available to me was great news, but it didn't magically solve my own leadership problems. It led me to deeper questions: If we have a choice and we know it, why do we keep responding in unproductive ways and experiencing such great difficulty? Why do even the most experienced or most successful leaders still sometimes feel backed into a corner with no way out?

It's because each of us gets tripped up by our deeply held assumptions about who we are as leaders and how we think we need to function in our role. As I discussed in *Own the Room*, my first book with coauthor Amy Jen Su, these assumptions, which are largely unconscious, tell us how to feel and think and behave. And especially when things get tough, they tend to block us from seeing the best course of action and the path of least resistance (and least suffering). In other words, when we get stuck and stress escalates, we tend to fall back on our default mechanisms for coping, which aren't always the most effective. I've come to think of these unconscious assumptions and limiting beliefs as *hidden blockers* because they keep us locked in unproductive patterns and unable to move forward, and they're so ingrained, so habitual, that they're experts at eluding detection.

When I was trying to make my division profitable all on my own, for instance, my belief that "I know I'm right" drove me to pursue my vision to the exclusion of all else. I was not open to others' input, and didn't realize I was damaging morale and undermining trust by not valuing my colleagues' ideas and insights. I was blocked by my idea of how I needed to lead.

And I'm not the only one. At some point or another, every leader goes through rough patches. (If you haven't yet, you will.) I've worked with thousands of leaders—from CEOs and other senior executives to frontline managers and high potentials—who have experienced success, often a lot of it, but have hit a wall. They've been chasing results that remain maddeningly out of reach, or they're wondering why they keep getting passed over for promotion. They're finding it difficult to connect with and influence people, or they're struggling to find their footing in a new role. Whatever the problem, they come to me for coaching with one thing in common: *something* is standing in the way of them reaching their most ambitious goals or of simply being the best leaders they want and know they can be. And despite their best efforts to overcome the obstacles, they're still blocked. Why?

Usually it's because they're focused in the wrong direction—on what's happening on the outside rather than on the inside. When they're facing a serious hurdle, a lot of high achievers (like me) think they can hustle their way through whatever is holding them back.

They turn to what's worked for them in the past, even if that approach doesn't work in this new situation. Many think they just need to make their way through the right checklist of tactics and skills to level up. And while taking outward actions like closing gaps in experience and attending training programs are valuable strategies that can help in the short term, they don't lead to the kind of change that will sustain a leader's performance over the long run. That kind of lasting change comes from within.

If you're feeling blocked and can't figure out how to get through the current impasse, then you're probably approaching your challenges in similar ways. You're caught up in how to deal with the circumstances around you and the people you have to work with. Don't get me wrong, these external factors are important and often contribute to the problem. But in my experience, leaders spend too much time and energy trying to control, manipulate, or cajole people into falling in line, and too much time stressing, ruminating, and plotting about how to force a situation to adhere to their expectations, when they should be focusing on the area where they have the most control: themselves.

Leaders receive a lot of training in the critical skills of managing others, influencing others, and providing feedback and direction to others. But they get little guidance on what to do when *they* are the reason they're stuck. I learned the hard way that until you shift your focus to what's happening within and discover and address the hidden blocker that's holding you back, you'll continue to struggle. You'll continue to feel that your goals are out of reach and that leadership is harder and more draining than it needs to be. You'll also continue to adversely affect the people you lead, in ways large and small, as the blockers prevent you from being the leader you're capable of being.

I've coached many people over the years, in my practice and as the host of the *Harvard Business Review* podcast *Coaching Real Leaders*, and I've found that the same is true for my clients: they think that someone or something else is to blame for their problems, but when we dig a little deeper, what we find in almost every case is a hidden blocker lurking beneath the surface:

- A general manager running a business unit of several thousand is compelled to solve every problem that comes along because, he assumes, "I can't make a mistake." This belief keeps him in the weeds, too busy to be strategic about his work or his career, and it prevents his team members from building the problem-solving skills they need to succeed on their own.

- A marketing executive struggles to build credibility after leaving a comfortable corporate gig for a startup. She's blocked from stepping up to lead in her challenging new role by the recurring thought of "I don't belong here."

- A principal at a consulting firm is having a hard time staffing his projects with high performers because he's built a reputation for being unfocused. His assumption of "I need it done now" drives him to tackle everything at once, rather than set priorities for his teams. Without attracting the best talent, his projects suffer, and he risks not making the critical promotion to partner.

I've now helped my clients uncover and break through these and many more hidden blockers so they're free to deal with their challenges more productively and effectively and, as they get the hang of the process, more efficiently and with greater ease. But not everyone has access to an executive coach, and most of us don't know how to coach ourselves. That's exactly why I've written this book. My hope is that *Leadership Unblocked* can function as your portable coach, a dependable and wise companion as you endeavor to become free of the blockers that are holding you back.

In this book, I'll show you how to identify your hidden blockers, and I'll offer you a roadmap with clearly delineated signposts to guide you in moving from blocked to unblocked. I'll share stories from and real conversations with leaders I've coached who've used this roadmap to get out of their own way and break through the hidden blockers hindering their personal development and career advancement.* Along the way we'll also look at research from the fields of psychology, neuroscience, business, and leadership, as well as enduring guidance from various wisdom teachings, that I offer to my own coaching clients.

We'll begin by looking at the impact of our beliefs on our behaviors, and I'll introduce you to the seven hidden blockers I've encountered most frequently in my work with leaders. I'll then guide you through a step-by-step process called the Blocked to Unblocked Roadmap that works for overcoming any hidden blocker. In chapters 3 through 9, we'll look at each of the seven common hidden blockers in detail, and you'll see how my clients broke through and moved on from the beliefs that were holding them back—and how you can too if you identify with that same limiting belief. Chapter 10 then focuses on what leaders can do to accelerate the inner growth of their employees so they are equipped to overcome *their* hidden blockers, and to help unblock from limiting beliefs that happen on an organizational level. Finally, I'll close with some guidance for the road ahead, and how you can use what you've learned moving forward.

A final word to the wise before we move on: though broadly speaking, coaching and therapy share similar aims of seeking to help individuals meet their goals, I want to be clear that coaching is not a substitute for therapy. During a coaching engagement, if I recognize that any limiting belief or pattern of thinking is getting in the way of a client's day-to-day living or overall well-being or is rooted in past trauma, I advise them to explore working with a licensed mental health professional, as I know and respect the bounds of my role as an executive coach. Similarly, this book is meant to support your professional growth, not function as a remedy for what may require

---

*Stories are based on actual executive coaching engagements with real leaders, though all identifying details, including but not limited to names, titles, and type of company and industry, have been changed in order to protect client confidentiality. Conversations have also been edited for length and clarity.

psychological, emotional, and even at times, physical healing. I also want to point out that executive coaching, or coaching of any kind, is not meant to be used as a means to cure or excuse toxic behavior, or as a way for organizations to protect toxic leaders. Rather, as you'll soon see, it requires a high level of self-awareness, ownership, and motivation to rectify any thinking patterns and behaviors that are blocking effective leadership. So as you read these pages, if you ever find yourself wondering whether working with a therapist would be helpful for you, I encourage you to check with your health-care provider.

It really can feel lonely and difficult at the top. But you don't have to suffer through your leadership challenges, nor should others have to suffer as a result of how you lead. Becoming free of your hidden blockers unlocks the potential not only for achieving your individual goals, delivering results for your organization, and leading with more ease, but for being the kind of visionary, high-impact leader so many of us long to be and, deep down, know we can be.

Chapter 1

What's Really Blocking You?

The mind is everything. What you think, you become.

—BUDDHA

Whether you realize it or not, your beliefs are constantly affecting how you think, feel, act, and view the world. Though we're seldom consciously aware of them as we go about our days, beliefs affect everything we do. They influence our decision-making and our values, the way we approach challenges and the way we solve problems, the way we learn and the way we lead. If we were to peel back the onion on every action and interaction, every emotion, every opinion and value judgment, and even our self-image and our memories, we'd find a belief at the center, exerting an influence in ways large or small.

Research from a wide array of fields attests to the undeniable power of our beliefs. Perhaps the most influential exploration of their effect on performance and achievement comes from Carol Dweck's pioneering work on mindset, the internal set of beliefs we have about ourselves. "Mindset permeates *every* part of your life," Dweck tells us, and "profoundly affects the way you lead your life. It can determine whether you become the person you want to be and whether you accomplish the things you value."[1] One of Dweck's key insights was linking belief to behavior and behavior to outcomes. She coined the terms "growth mindset" and "fixed mindset" to describe two overarching types of beliefs that people have about where their abilities come from and how those beliefs determine success and achievement.

People with a growth mindset believe that their abilities and intelligence can be developed and improved through effort, learning, and perseverance. They're willing to put in effort, take risks, and persist in the face of obstacles because they think their actions will have a positive effect. They are high in what's known as self-efficacy, or the belief in your ability to achieve a task or meet a goal. Self-efficacy has been linked with high motivation, academic achievement, athletic and professional performance, and organizational success. And really, it's no wonder: because growth-oriented individuals have confidence in their ability to succeed, they set higher goals for themselves, put in more effort, and persist longer on difficult tasks, which they view as surmountable challenges rather than cause for giving up. They focus on opportunities worth pursuing rather than on risks to avoid. In short, they expect to do well—and then they put in the effort to make those results happen.[2] Their positive results confirm their belief, creating a positive feedback loop or virtuous cycle.

Those with a fixed mindset and low self-efficacy, on the other hand, believe that their abilities and intelligence are carved in stone and unchangeable, and that whatever actions they take to improve themselves won't make an appreciable difference. They doubt their ability to handle difficulties and challenging situations, and tend to give up when they encounter obstacles. Thus they also tend to shy away from stretch goals and challenges they perceive to be difficult. They are more prone to discount positive thoughts and experiences and focus instead on negative thoughts and experiences, which can easily result in a vicious cycle of negative thoughts begetting negative behavior and negative outcomes—the classic self-fulfilling prophecy.

What Is a Belief?

At its simplest, a belief is the conviction that something is true, regardless of the evidence. Beliefs can exist in our conscious mind, where we can see and be aware of them, or they can exist in the subconscious, influencing our perceptions and behaviors without our awareness.

Beliefs are formed in two main ways: by accepting information from an authoritative source as truth, or by making inferences and deductions based on our own observations. Many of the core beliefs we carry into adulthood and into the workplace are rooted in the assumptions and viewpoints we learned early on from our family, caregivers, and surrounding culture.

Scientists tell us that beliefs provide a "mental scaffolding" that helps us interpret and appraise our environment and our experiences, explain new observations, and construct a shared meaning of the world.[a] Beliefs play such a large part in how we interpret and make sense of things that it can feel threatening to have them challenged by contradictory evidence or have them questioned—even if we're the ones doing the questioning. This helps explain why it can be very difficult to move on from a core belief.

a. Michael H. Connors and Peter W. Halligan, "A Cognitive Account of Belief: A Tentative Road Map," *Frontiers in Psychology* 5 (2015), https://doi.org/10.3389/fpsyg.2014.01588.

If you still have any doubt as to whether your beliefs impact your outcomes, just take a look at some of the research from cognitive and behavioral psychology. Stanford professor and psychologist Alia Crum studied a group of hotel room attendants who were on their feet and moving throughout the day. When asked if they exercised, most of the attendants said no, because they didn't think of the physical activity associated with their jobs as working *out*; they thought of it as work. But simply introducing the idea that their work was also good exercise resulted in physiological changes. After just four weeks of shifting from the belief that "work is work" to the belief that "work is good exercise," the room attendants showed a decrease in weight, blood pressure, body fat, waist-to-hip ratio, and body mass index.[3] "Objective health benefits, things like a healthy heart and a healthy weight," Crum concluded, "depend not just on what we're doing but what we *think* about what we do." Mindset, she says, is not peripheral or inconsequential. It is central to behavior.[4]

Whether we're aware of them or not, our beliefs have concrete and immediate effects on our health, happiness, and professional success. With so much importance riding on them, and so much at stake for ourselves and those we lead, we'd all benefit from taking a closer look at how our beliefs can help or hinder how we lead.

Supportive versus Limiting Beliefs

While beliefs themselves are neutral, neither good nor bad, some beliefs limit us while others support us. Limiting beliefs are the thoughts and assumptions we hold about ourselves, others, or our context that hold us back, undermine our performance, and frustrate our attempts to reach our goals. If you have limiting thoughts—assumptions that work against you rather than for you—you will have limited results. As I write this book, for example, if the thought that dominates my mind is "No one will want to read this. Why should I even bother?" it will slow down my writing, if not stall it altogether. The result I will get is procrastination rather than productivity (and possibly poor writing).

Supportive beliefs are just the opposite. They're the thoughts and assumptions that give us confidence in our abilities, enhance our performance, and propel us toward our goals. If you start with a supportive belief that's aligned with the results you want, it will get you to your desired destination more quickly, and with greater ease. If my dominant belief while writing is "I know this book will help people. I will put my best effort into writing it and it will resonate with who it needs to," that frees me up to write without holding back.

In his book *Positive Intelligence*, Shirzad Chamine captures what so many of us have experienced: "Your mind is your best friend. But it is also your worst enemy." The goal, he says, is to optimize how much your mind acts in your interest rather than in ways that undermine your efforts. "What percentage of time is your mind serving you vs. sabotaging you?"[5] he asks. In order to make that determination, you have to recognize when you are holding beliefs that limit you so you can shift to the ones that support you.

Understanding your beliefs turns out to be trickier than you'd think, though, because the majority of your beliefs aren't conscious. Until you become aware of them, you can't truly understand why you do what you do.

Not long ago, my life partner and I began hearing a steady drip-drip-drip coming from our bathroom. For a while we engaged in the kind of magical thinking so many busy homeowners do (we hoped the situation would somehow go away on its own), but soon the drips were a waterfall. We tried to tighten the washers, we fiddled with the faucets, and we even went so far as to replace the shower-head. No luck. The source of the problem was coming from somewhere we couldn't see. Until we opened up the wall and inspected the plumbing behind it, we wouldn't know the true cause of the leak, and it certainly couldn't be resolved.

Working with the unconscious is a little like that. We have easy access to what we can observe externally—our own behaviors and their impact—but becoming aware of the beliefs that drive those behaviors requires us to look deeper, behind the wall.

The other very tricky part of knowing our beliefs is how often they're not actually truthful. While we may like to think that our beliefs are based on verifiable facts, they are quite often based on our *interpretation* of the facts. And unfortunately, interpretation is fertile soil for misperceptions, mistaken assumptions, unconscious biases, or faulty reasoning. This is why there is a difference between what you see (fact) and the story you tell yourself about it (belief). Cognitive scientists tell us that we're far more likely to form a belief *first* and look for supporting evidence later. Once a belief is formed, we're also reluctant to change it. When we're presented with contradictory evidence, we tend to stick with our original belief and search for new "evidence" to support it—even if it's illogical or directly inhibiting our progress.[6]

This is not because we're delusional or hopelessly irrational. It's because our brains are hardwired to look for patterns amid the deluge of information and sensory input we must process on a daily basis, and as an energy-hungry organ, our brains will do whatever it takes to conserve energy. Thus we see patterns and create storylines that help us organize and interpret our experience, we're selective in what we pay attention to, and we take mental shortcuts that speed up our ability to make decisions and take action. These mental processes all happen within seconds, and usually without our conscious awareness. This is great for efficient mental functioning and just getting things done every day. But those patterns and storylines may or may not reflect reality and, as a result, may misdirect our actions.

Let's make this concrete. Picture a meeting where the boss rushes in late, clearly frazzled and agitated. One employee thinks, "Oh no, she's mad at me," and starts mentally cataloging all the things he could've missed or done wrong to make his boss angry. Another thinks, "Oh no, she's overwhelmed, and I need to jump in," and starts speculating on what the problem could be and how they can solve it. A third thinks, "Oh no, there must be a problem at home," and wonders if it's appropriate to ask about it. These are three wildly different interpretations based on the exact same input—and who knows if any of them is even close to accurate.

We do this all the time. We constantly tell ourselves stories in order to make sense of our experience and determine a path forward. It happens automatically and instantaneously, and unless we pause to examine those stories, we could be basing our decisions and actions on mistaken assumptions, which then will lead to unproductive decisions and misplaced actions.

This is why awareness is everything. It's why we need to shine a light on what's happening with our thinking. Otherwise, we will continue to operate on autopilot, unconsciously letting our limiting beliefs remain in the driver's seat, compromising our leadership.

With awareness, however, we realize that we don't have to settle for beliefs that don't support us. Beliefs may *feel* permanent and immutable, but science assures us that they are not. They can evolve over time as we're exposed to a widening circle of influences or if we actively do the work to change them.

With the awareness that beliefs are malleable, we can even deliberately choose experiences and thoughts that affect our beliefs—and our outcomes—in a desired way. Research in neuroplasticity, or the ability of the brain to form new neural connections in response to experience, firmly establishes that the brain continues to develop throughout our lifespan. What we thought was hardwired can indeed be rewired—and yes, that even applies to a fixed mindset and your most firmly entrenched beliefs. "Although the initial wiring of our brains is based on early experience," notes author and psychotherapist Linda Graham, "we know that later experiences, especially healthy relational ones, can undo or overwrite that early learning to help us cope differently and more resiliently with anything, anything at all."[7] We can even deliberately choose actions, beliefs, and thought patterns in a way that best supports the leadership goals we set for ourselves. According to neuroscience and organizational behavior professor Justin James Kennedy, leadership development programs and organizations that incorporate principles of neuroplasticity, such as exposure to new situations and concepts and the ability to practice responding to them in a supportive environment, will produce leaders who are better able to adapt and to learn quickly how to manage a team in an unpredictable environment.[8]

Simply realizing that beliefs aren't set in stone has been profoundly liberating for many of my clients. But it's just the beginning. To consciously pick our beliefs and align them with how we want to lead, we first need to identify exactly which beliefs support our growth, goals, and effectiveness, and which ones are keeping us stuck and unable to move forward.

Uncovering Your Limiting Beliefs

Unsure of what your beliefs are? Pause for a moment and listen to your interior monologue—that voice inside your head. Most of us have a constant backdrop of mental chatter going on, also known as self-talk, that we don't often consciously pay attention to. Much of this chatter is neutral; you think about things you need to do, you rehearse a future conversation, you play back a recent situation. But a lot of the time, our self-talk can be harsh or critical, and when that happens, chances are there's a limiting belief behind that self-criticism: "I'll never finish this." "Who do you think you are, setting your sights on that role?" "Any minute now, they'll find out I'm a fraud." If we're not aware of the chatter that's going on, our negative and critical self-talk can sabotage our mood and undermine our performance, and we won't even know what's behind it.

Even as I sit here and write this chapter, if I pay attention to my interior monologue, I can hear limiting beliefs popping up that are working against me. *What you're writing doesn't make sense. Others have already written better leadership books. You'll never be able to turn all your material into a book, much less one that people will want to read.*

Yup—welcome to my world! This litany of limiting beliefs has all come up in just the last hour, and it's making the process of writing feel like carrying a fifty-pound backpack while running uphill. But I get it. These thoughts are actually trying to help me—even to protect me.

Let me illustrate how my limiting thoughts are trying to be help-ful. To do that, we need to go back in time. As early as I can remember, I believed that the better I performed—the more A's I got, the more accolades I received, the more spelling bee trophies I won—the more valued I would be. That unless I was the best at what I did, it was not worth it. Those beliefs didn't come out of nowhere. I don't know their exact starting point, but there's plenty of evidence for how they could have formed. I remember running for student council vice president in high school and cheerfully sharing my victory with my parents. To which they responded, "That's great, Muriel. But why didn't you run for president?" I now understand that this was my parents' way of saying they believed I could do whatever I put my mind to and hoped I wasn't selling myself short. But in my fourteen-year-old mind, all I could hear was, "VP is not good enough. *You* are not good enough unless you reach the top. We will only be happy when you are the best." Oy, is it any surprise that left to my own devices, there is a part of my thinking that still goes to "If you can't be the best at something, it's not worth it" to keep me from feeling the letdown I felt that day, even though that day happened so long ago? Often, our limiting thoughts aren't based on what is happening in the here and now but arise to protect us from reexperiencing something that happened in the past.

The mind is so hardwired to insulate us from harm that we form adaptive strategies very early in life. We figure out who we need to be and what we need to believe to feel safe in our environment, to feel seen and accepted, and to feel worthy, all of which is perfectly understandable. These are critical human needs, after all. After the basic physiological needs of air, water, food, shelter, clothing, and sleep, psychologist Abraham Maslow identified the next levels of human needs:

- *Safety:* to feel protected

- *Belonging:* to feel connected

- *Esteem:* to feel worthwhile

When we don't get those needs met, we unconsciously figure out how to get them met through external means—through relationships, family, and guess what? Work and achievement. For me, the belief that "I must be the best in order to feel accepted and worthwhile" drove my accomplishments, which met those needs for belonging and esteem by winning me praise and approval. It also prevented me from feeling the sting of disapproval.

But at what cost? Every time I won the praise and approval I was seeking, it reinforced my belief that I needed to achieve in order to feel accepted and worthwhile, which sent me on an endless quest to constantly up my game. But I never felt like I'd fully arrived, because the warm feelings only lasted so long. Soon I needed to be the best at something else to feel worthy again, and I was off in pursuit of the next win. I'm sure many of you can relate.

Now, present-day Muriel knows that this belief isn't truly help-ful—I am no longer a teenager running for student council, and my sense of belonging and worth is not predicated on my achievements. But notice how that belief still exists and comes rushing out when I'm faced with the fear of not being the best. The big difference now is that I am aware of this limiting belief and know when it arises. Now I don't have to let it block me. In fact, I can even be grateful for it, because I recognize that it's trying to protect me. It's still, bless its pointy little head, laboring to get my needs met and trying to prevent the hurt I'd feel if my work isn't well received. This is why I will never denigrate a belief itself, even if it's limiting or outright harm-ful, because somewhere, deep down, it's trying to serve a protective purpose. It may miss the mark or cause unintended difficulty, but it's trying to address a deep need and provide a benefit.

That said, recognizing the good intention of a belief that is block-ing you does not mean you surrender the microphone to it. If it's no longer useful or if it's impeding your progress, it's time to change your thinking. Unless we uncover, unpack, and unblock from the hidden blockers that get in the way of meeting our potential, we can very well end up like Sisyphus—pushing the rock up the mountain the same way over and over again, only to see it roll back down every time before we reach the top.

Seven Common Hidden Blockers

Throughout more than twenty years of helping leaders achieve their professional goals, the same unhelpful thought patterns seemed to come up so often among clients that I decided to take a closer look. I conducted an in-depth analysis of over three hundred of my coaching clients from many different industries, backgrounds, and levels of experience, and sure enough, the same patterns of unexamined assumptions and unproductive beliefs came up again and again. Though there's no shortage of hidden blockers, in this book we're going to focus on the ones I saw occurring most often. Seven primary hidden blockers made that short list. These are so common that if something is impeding your progress and keeping you from leading at your fullest potential, you'll likely find the culprit among them:

1. *"I need to be involved"*: the belief that you need to be part of every detail at every level

2. *"I need it done now"*: the belief that you need to get results right away, no matter what

3. *"I know I'm right"*: the belief that you—and only you—know the answers to the problems at hand

4. *"I can't make a mistake"*: the belief that your performance must be flawless, above reproach

5. *"If I can do it, so can you"*: the belief that others' performance must be like yours to be acceptable

6. *"I can't say no"*: the belief that you must say yes and step up to the plate when asked

7. *"I don't belong here"*: the belief that you don't fit in where you are or at your level

It's not unusual to be affected by more than one hidden blocker at once. But I've found that it's most beneficial to address one limiting belief at a time—namely, the *primary* blocker that's currently standing in the way of your leadership goals. With some practice and the process you'll learn in this book, you can be your own coach to identify which of your beliefs are hindering rather than helping, and then zero in on the one that's taken over and leading to unintended impact.

Let me assure you, the work to unblock from your hidden blockers is absolutely worth it. You no longer have to live at the mercy of your unexamined, unproductive beliefs and the ineffective actions that grow out of them. You have more control and autonomy over your current situation and your future goals than you think. Your beliefs, and therefore your actions and outcomes, can be deliberate, empowering, and aligned with your goals, rather than unreflective, unproductive, and limiting.

If all this sounds good to you, then it's time to break free of your limiting beliefs and get unblocked.

Chapter 2

How to Get Out of Your Own Way

Watch your thoughts, they become your words; watch your words, they become your actions; watch your actions, they become your habits; watch your habits, they become your character; watch your character, it becomes your destiny.

—LAO TZU

While getting to know ourselves and understanding the beliefs that hold us back is a critical first step, the real magic happens when we're able to free ourselves of limiting beliefs and achieve different results. To help you do that, I've distilled what I've learned from coaching and helping clients break free of their hidden blockers into a guide called the Blocked to Unblocked Roadmap (see figure 2-1).

As you can see, the Blocked to Unblocked Roadmap consists of three stages that are divided into two steps each. It's important that you complete the steps in order, as each one builds on the last to help you uncover and unpack the primary hidden blocker that's currently holding you back and, ultimately, shift to a belief that will move you from blocked to unblocked. Let me walk you through each stage and step, and then in subsequent chapters you'll see how

FIGURE 2-1

Blocked to Unblocked Roadmap

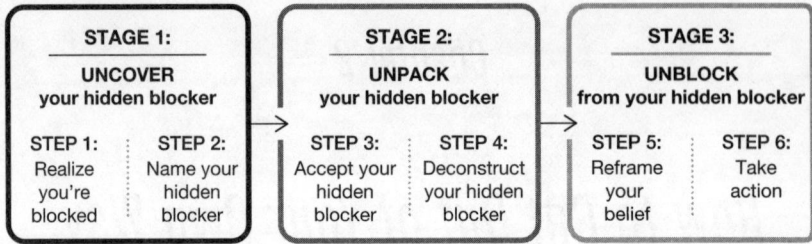

STAGE 1:		STAGE 2:		STAGE 3:	
UNCOVER your hidden blocker		UNPACK your hidden blocker		UNBLOCK from your hidden blocker	
STEP 1: Realize you're blocked	STEP 2: Name your hidden blocker	STEP 3: Accept your hidden blocker	STEP 4: Deconstruct your hidden blocker	STEP 5: Reframe your belief	STEP 6: Take action

the whole process works with each of the seven most common hidden blockers.

Stage One: Uncover Your Hidden Blocker

Stage one begins with paying attention to your own experience and acknowledging that *something* is off. That signal can be subtle and ill-defined (you feel tense, frustrated, or unmotivated at work but you're not sure why), or it can be obvious and specific (you keep getting passed for promotion or you receive negative feedback). Whatever it is, your results aren't lining up with your expectations, and you know you need to make a change.

Awareness is important because without it there is no impetus to do anything differently. But research shows that even though most of us believe we're self-aware, only 10 percent to 15 percent of people actually are.[1] So the goal of stage one is to become aware of *what* is happening. And we do this by taking an honest look at our behavior.

Step One: Realize You're Blocked

Step one is about recognizing your action and acknowledging its impact. Many times, we're not aware of what we're doing or the effect

Signs You Are Blocked

Being blocked isn't always obvious. Here are a few signs indicating that you could be hindered by a hidden blocker.

Internal signs

I feel stuck.

I feel frustrated.

I feel chronically dissatisfied at work.

I feel emotionally or mentally exhausted.

I feel uncharacteristically cynical or negative about work.

I feel less effective than usual.

I feel out of options, like I'm backed into a corner.

I feel resentment toward some of my colleagues.

I feel a lot of angst or tension when I think about work.

I know something needs to change.

External signs

I was blindsided by a negative performance review.

I received feedback that doesn't line up with how I see myself.

I'm unable to achieve results through others like I used to.

My team's morale is low.

My career advancement has stalled.

I'm not receiving buy-in from leadership.

I am not able to keep up with the demands of the job.

I don't have the bandwidth to add value at a strategic level.

My intent is frequently misunderstood.

our actions are having—on others, on ourselves, and on the objectives we're trying to reach.

Take, for example, my experience of single-handedly trying to save the underperforming division at my corporate job. I was convinced my actions were exactly what was needed to turn the division around—and that the reason I wasn't getting the results I expected was because my team wasn't following my orders. I blamed everyone else for why we weren't moving forward. It was only after many months of frustration and not achieving my goals that I hit a wall and was startled into the awareness that maybe I was part of the problem—if not *the* problem. At last, I became conscious of my own behavior and its impact on my colleagues and our lack of progress.

Step one often requires a tough-love approach, especially when our actions reflect poorly on us or don't square with our self-image. I was deeply wedded to my sense of being an overachiever who excelled at everything she took on. And until that point, that's exactly what my track record reflected, so when I hit one obstacle after another, it just did not compute. My lack of progress *must* be another's fault, right?

It's natural to want to explain, defend, or make excuses for our actions—or to blame others for them, which lets us off the hook and shifts the responsibility for creating *and* resolving the situation to someone else. But step one is about observing the unvarnished facts. It asks us to focus exclusively on our actions and their natural consequences, putting aside all justifications, rationalizations, explanations, interpretations, contributing factors, background contexts, and excuses. There may indeed be understandable reasons you behaved the way you did, but for now, we're spotlighting your behavior. Your task is to gain awareness—to come face-to-face with the situation and see it for what it is.

So how do we do this? We stick to the cold, hard facts. We see our actions and their impact for what they are—nothing more and nothing less.

Step Two: Name Your Hidden Blocker

Once we're aware of our behavior—yep, I did that—it's time to shift the focus from the external to the internal and start trying to name the hidden blocker—the belief—that's powering the unwanted behavior. Sometimes we may be keenly aware of the limiting belief that's blocking us, but more often it takes a little work, and perhaps even multiple attempts, before we can see and then correctly name a hidden blocker. This is why I tell leaders to cut themselves some slack and approach this as they would a brainstorming session. At first, we're just going to do a little hypothesizing. We're going to try out some contenders to see what fits.

It's worth getting it right because there is great power in accurately naming something. In ancient myths across many cultures, calling an adversary by name lends one power and control over it, and modern science offers its own version of this timeless tale. Neuroimaging studies have found that naming negative emotions—what scientists refer to as affect labeling—helps us manage difficult emotional states and regain control.[2] Similarly, naming our hidden blocker achieves two goals:

1. *We can objectify it.* We get some distance between ourselves and the belief that's holding us back, and we take back some of the control we lost when we were acting without awareness. We realize that "I am not this belief, I just *hold* this belief, which means it is not an inextricable part of my identity and I can let it go."

2. *We can actually talk about it and work with it.* Naming a hidden blocker brings the unconscious into the conscious, where we can discuss it, examine it, critique it—and eventually change it.

Accurately naming a blocker can be much harder than you'd think, though, because it's so common to think of blockers as *behaviors*, rather than the beliefs that are driving the behavior. There are a million and one reasons we often confuse the two, but mainly they boil down to two sides of the same coin: a bias toward action and a resistance toward introspection.

I'm speaking broadly here, but ambitious, high-performing leaders who have built careers upon achieving, fixing, problem-solving, and strategizing are very accustomed to *doing*. And no wonder. When it comes to sheer execution, action rules the day. It's how we get so much done, solve so many problems, and garner so many wins. But an overemphasis on action can also fool us into thinking self-reflection is a waste of time. Research shows us nothing could be further from the truth. Leaders who engage in regular self-reflection exhibit greater emotional intelligence, enhanced connection with their company's vision and mission, and better problem-solving skills, and are better able to manage and inspire their teams.[3] They also make more progress toward their goals and have higher self-esteem on the days they engage in self-reflective activities, such as writing about their positive leadership qualities.[4] Having a strong bias for action can also lead you to jump into developing solutions before you fully understand the problem—and in this case, your problem is your beliefs.[5]

Our reluctance to engage in self-reflection is often also rooted in fear. It's not exactly fun to face our vulnerabilities or any uncomfortable realities about ourselves. They may seem beyond our control to change, and there's always the fear that if we open the can of worms, we might not be able to get them back into the can so we can go about our business. Let me assure you, though, that avoiding the hidden blocker actually reinforces it.

Stage Two: Unpack Your Hidden Blocker

Once a leader knows they're blocked and has named their hidden blocker, stage two gets into why it is present. It's all about gaining an understanding of the personal reasons behind this hidden blocker and then doing the deeper work necessary to become unblocked from it.

The goal of stage two is to understand *why* all of this is happening.

Step Three: Accept Your Hidden Blocker

It's one thing to see the signs that you're blocked, but it's another to own them. You can't move forward unless you can accept how your thinking affects what you do—without blaming others—and own up to the ramifications a hidden blocker is having on you, your colleagues, and your organization.

I want to be very clear about what I mean by acceptance. I'm talking about acknowledging that your hidden blocker is present and that it is affecting you and the people around you. It does *not* mean resigning yourself to the situation ("I guess this is just the way I am"), beating yourself up for it ("I hate that I think this way"), or, again, trying to deny, defend, justify, or rationalize it away.

Acceptance of your hidden blocker means you don't deny or resist the situation you're in. Resisting the reality of the situation is where most of our suffering comes from—and where our leadership becomes compromised and our efforts counterproductive. It's the quickest way to remain a hostage to your unhelpful belief and blocked in the unproductive behavior it engenders. The more I refused to accept that my peers were not buying into my plans for the division, the more I pushed for my agenda—and the more they pushed back. If I had not resisted the reality of the situation, I would have listened to their concerns and tried to understand and address them. It's only with acceptance that we can take responsibility for our own contribution to the problem and make positive strides toward change. Otherwise, we'll just continue foisting the blame onto external causes and waiting around for something to change. And this is not to absolve any external causes—underperforming team members, toxic bosses, insufficient resources, or systemic bias, for example—and their contribution to the situation. This is to accept and own what part *you* play and how you respond to external circumstances, because that is all you really can control.

Step Four: Deconstruct Your Hidden Blocker

Step four is the part in the process where we go deeper. This is where we engage in some introspection, reflect on our experiences, and look at the origins of the hidden blocker that's been holding us back, what purpose it's serving, and why we hold on to it so tightly. This step helps us kick the tires of our own assumptions and see if our belief has any merit.

Many times, simply uncovering the origins of a hidden blocker goes a long way in dismantling it and diminishing its hold. Sometimes during this step, though, a client discovers that the origin of their hidden blocker is based on trauma or other experiences they have difficulty dealing with. In that case, many choose to work with a therapist, as healing from the past goes beyond the scope of leadership coaching. Indeed, it is not uncommon for leaders to engage in coaching in conjunction with counseling or other therapeutic outlets, and these forms of support can be wonderfully complementary.

Deconstructing our hidden blockers can be challenging, so I encourage clients to approach this task with patience, open-minded curiosity, and self-compassion, and to use whatever methods work best to deepen their self-awareness. For many, it's writing down their reflections. Some leaders ask a friend to listen as they talk through their thoughts and ask questions to help deepen their responses. In team coaching, I ask peers to share their responses with each other. When one person is sharing, the others listen and ask more questions. It's amazing how much they unpack about their beliefs in a short period of time. Whatever you do, don't bypass this step in the process by skipping your own introspection. Otherwise, the unblock you want in the next step won't happen.

Stage Three: Unblock from Your Hidden Blocker

We've now arrived at the stage everyone wants to jump to: action. This is often where my clients want to start; they want to know what to *do*. But once they go through the process of uncovering their hidden blocker and understanding its impact, they realize that any effort to do something differently without the mindset shift would be short-lived. Stage three is where the magic really happens because it's where we choose what to do and how to act rather than succumb to a default behavior. My clients find that this stage gives them a sense of power and control, because they're choosing what's happening next, rather than living at the mercy of unexamined thoughts and beliefs that remain buried in the subconscious, influencing their behavior and undermining their efforts. It's the point in the process to knit back together what has become disconnected, to align our thoughts with a desired outcome.

The goal of stage three is to act out of full awareness and mindfully *choose* how we want to act.

Step Five: Reframe Your Belief

The main order of business in step five is to reframe our belief so that it aligns with what we want to happen in the future. If I want to show up at work with confidence and gravitas, for example, I can't hang on to the belief that I'm not good enough or that I don't belong. Holding those beliefs internally will never add up to me showing up with confidence externally . . . at least not for long. Instead, I need a strong, supportive belief that will counteract my blocker and function as the springboard for getting me to my desired outcome. Reframing our belief is a very conscious and deliberate step that puts us in the driver's seat. It reclaims the agency and autonomy that living under the influence of a hidden blocker has taken, and it enables us to adapt moving forward.

The best way to choose a more helpful belief is to work back from your desired outcomes. Our hidden blockers are subconscious beliefs that are grounded in the past. They keep us locked in old, unproductive ways of doing things; they're why you're here right now, in need of a change. Helpful, supportive beliefs, on the other hand, are based on a clear, conscious perception of what's happening now and what you'd like to happen in the future. They are, by nature, forward-thinking.

The best way to free ourselves is to align our thinking with what we want to happen, and—this is important—in a way that resonates and will stick. Let's take a look at some coaching questions that can help you reframe your belief.

- What is the current impact you're having as a result of being blocked?

- What is the impact you want to have?

- In order to move from blocked to unblocked, what belief do you need to let go of because it keeps you stuck in your blocked state?

- What belief could you pick up that would support and sustain your unblocked state?

By clarifying what you want your impact to be, you can articulate a belief that would get you there and move away from the one that was holding you back. That's how you *unblock* yourself from your blocker: by reframing it to a belief that is authentic to you and that's aligned to your vision of the leader you want to be.

Step Six: Take Action

The final step in the Blocked to Unblocked Roadmap is to define and commit to a set of actions that can make your intended impact come to life. This is where it all comes together. All the work will enable you to reach a new state, one from which you can take wise, informed action, rather than act unconsciously out of hidden blockers and fears. When our actions don't line up with what we think, we experience a discomfort called cognitive dissonance—that feeling when we're not walking our own talk. And in this case, the "talk" is the new belief. The risk with cognitive dissonance is that you adapt your thinking to justify the actions, thereby increasing the chances that you go right back to the beliefs that were hindering you in the first place. It's very important that we don't just claim a different way of thinking, but that we also adopt actions and behaviors that reinforce our unblocked mindset. There is a self-fulfilling prophecy in action here; beliefs lead to actions and actions reinforce beliefs.[6] For example, it's not enough to believe that "valuing what other people say is important." You have to follow that up with the action of listening to make it stick. Your actions can now be deliberate and specific, fully aligned with your leadership goal, and powered by your new belief.

It's time to take all that inner work and put it into practice with action. What specific steps will you take to help you move from blocked to unblocked? What actions best line up with the strong, supportive belief that will enable you to lead the way you want to and achieve your desired future? By simply listing what you should *start doing* and *stop doing* you'll be on your way to seeing the results of your new mindset.

From Blocked to Unblocked

The process that's captured in the Blocked to Unblocked Roadmap is straightforward, but that doesn't mean the work is easy or that progress happens in a straight line. Hidden blockers are sneaky. Overcoming them will take time, effort, and discipline. But if you follow the steps in the process to uncover your hidden blocker, unpack it, and unblock yourself from it, you'll be able to recognize it the next time it rears its head. We all fall back into old patterns from time to time. The difference is that after you become aware of your hidden blockers and have learned to coach yourself through them, you won't be thrown off course for long.

No matter how intractable your blockers seem or what leadership obstacles you're experiencing, you don't have to remain stuck, hindered from leading at your fullest potential. You can thrive—and thus your teams and organizations can thrive—when you learn how to get out of your own way. The Blocked to Unblocked Roadmap gives you a reliable tool for doing just that.

Starting with the next chapter, we're going to examine each of the seven most common hidden blockers one by one. You'll see how real leaders in various contexts and career stages got unblocked from the limiting beliefs and unproductive behaviors that were hampering their growth and frustrating their sense of ease and accomplishment—and ultimately, how each one was able to move from blocked to unblocked. My advice is to read every chapter even if you think a hidden blocker won't apply to you, because, as we've seen, many limiting beliefs exist subconsciously, which makes them difficult to detect. But seeing how they affect others can be the mirror you need to increase your self-awareness.

As you make your way through these next seven chapters, see if you recognize yourself in any of these leaders' stories. If you find that a story particularly resonates with you, take note of how this leader moved from blocked to unblocked, so you can start imagining how you can do the same. The Coach Yourself section at the end of each chapter will give you a snapshot view of how to reframe that particular hidden blocker and move to action. Then when you're ready for the deeper work, you can use the Blocked to Unblocked Roadmap and the questions you'll find in the appendix to coach yourself through your own hidden blocker, in the same way I coached the leaders in these chapters. The sooner you start the process, the sooner you too can move from being blocked to unblocked.

Part Two

The Hidden Blockers

Chapter 3

I Need to Be Involved

We think, mistakenly, that success is the result of the
amount of time we put in at work, instead of the quality
of time we put in.

—ARIANNA HUFFINGTON

After building his investment banking career on Wall Street, Alex
was now the chief financial officer (CFO) of a reputable investment
management firm. He had been wanting to work with an executive
coach ever since landing this role a year before, and he'd gotten my
name from a good friend of his I'd coached.

Our kickoff meeting took place at his company's downtown office. As I sat in the conference room waiting for him, I found myself
counting the minutes past our scheduled start time. Five, ten, fifteen
minutes went by before Alex hurried in, talking on his mobile. He
gave me a wave and a smile as he told the person on the other end
that he really had to go but would follow up at first opportunity.

"Sorry to keep you waiting," Alex said. "Another fire to put out.
Can I get you some coffee?"

"No worries. These things happen," I said. "I'm good. Why don't
you get what you need and catch your breath before we start?" I wanted

to put him at ease. As Alex poured himself some coffee (it was 10:15 a.m., and this was his third cup), we chatted a bit to get to know each other better before diving in.

When I first meet with a coaching client, they are usually at one of three starting points: (1) they know what they need to work on, (2) they *think* they know what they need to work on but are focused on the wrong thing, or (3) they have no idea what they need to work on. I was eager to see which camp Alex fell into.

"So, what's going on, Alex?" I asked. "Can you tell me more about what you're hoping to get from coaching?"

"Well, everyone I respect and trust and who's doing well in their career has worked with a coach," he said. "So, I just figured it's something I should do."

"Well, I'm glad they've all had positive experiences," I said, "but getting a coach because everyone else has isn't a good reason to have one. Typically, my clients have something going on that's making them think they'd benefit from working with me. Let's figure out if I can help. Otherwise, this will just be a series of nice conversations, and you don't need to hire me to have those. You started this job a little over a year ago. How are things going so far?"

Alex told me that in many respects, this was the opportunity of a lifetime. As CFO he could help shape the direction of the company. It was his first chance to lead at a higher, broader level and have a much larger strategic impact, which is what he wanted. That all sounded great, and I told him so, but when I asked him to describe some of the specific ways in which he was getting to play this expanded strategic role, Alex sighed.

"That's the issue," he said. "It's not really happening, and I'm frustrated that I haven't been able to do the very thing I came here to do."

"What's getting in your way?" I asked.

"Who has the time? I don't even have time to eat lunch, let alone think about the future financial strategy of this firm," he said.

"So, you want to be a strategic leader. But you don't have the time."

"You've got it," Alex said with a laugh. "Can you help me find more time in my day?"

Alex was not unique in thinking that not having enough time was preventing him from leading at a higher level. Most of us have busier schedules than we'd like, but having more time is not what necessarily leads to being more strategic. I asked Alex how he was using the time he had.

"I'm constantly in meetings," he said. "On calls. On Zooms. I mean, you heard me when I came in—I was finishing up my fourth meeting of the day . . . and it's still early. It's nonstop. Here, take a look at my calendar."

Sure enough, the schedule Alex pulled up on his phone was jam-packed. He wasn't exaggerating about not having time for lunch—there was no white space in his calendar, and on many days, there were overlapping meetings. I asked him to tell me more about those meetings.

"Well, a lot of them are with my direct reports to go over what they're working on," he said. "Then there are team meetings I attend just to stay on top of the work happening downstream to make sure it's being done right. I also attend several committee meetings because I don't want the discussions to go too far before I weigh in. Let's see . . . there's a bunch of calls with external stakeholders I dial into just to be sure I'm there to answer questions if my direct reports can't handle them. We're also in the process of hiring associates, so I'm meeting with HR a lot to talk about the candidates, and I'm vetting résumés. Then I'm sitting in on the daily investor relations check-ins because that team is prepping for our annual meeting. I'm not sure why some of these other meetings are here, but people put things in my calendar all the time."

Alex went on and on about his meetings and how busy they kept him—so busy they prevented him from "being strategic." He was so caught up in his packed days, he wasn't able to take an aerial view of his situation and discern whether he was playing any role in hindering his efforts to be a strategic leader.

Alex Uncovers His Hidden Blocker

If Alex had come to coaching with more awareness, he would have sensed a tension: that instead of spending his time and energy on the high-value activities that were expected of him and that had attracted him to the position in the first place—things like focusing on strategy, building external relationships, and developing his people—he was down in the minutiae because of his own choices. Looking at himself and asking, "How am I contributing to this issue?" was the last thing on his mind.

For all of us, recognizing what's really going on is the first step toward change. According to Greg McKeown, leadership consultant and author of *Essentialism: The Disciplined Pursuit of Less*, the goal for leaders should be to operate at their "highest point of contribution by doing only what is essential."[1] Alex is hardly the only leader who has struggled to identify high-level priorities and make the best use of his time. Ironically, the more success we experience, the more opportunities and options we receive, and the harder it can become to keep our effort clearly aligned with our goals.

Alex felt like he wasn't doing the work that had attracted him to the role, yet he hadn't made any changes, so our first task would be to increase his awareness by assessing his situation. I invited him to complete a simple exercise. First, I asked him to list the ways he wanted to spend his time as CFO. Alex had no trouble defining the contributions he wanted to make and quickly wrote them on the meeting room whiteboard (pictured in table 3-1).

Next, I asked Alex to write out how he was actually spending his time. Visually comparing the two lists made it impossible to ignore that low-value activities were eating up the time and energy he should have been devoting to the work that would really benefit him, his team, and the organization. Asking himself, "Am I engaging at the

TABLE 3-1

What Alex wants to do versus what Alex is doing

How I want to spend my time	How I'm actually spending my time
• Working with the CEO to shape the firm's agenda by defining investment strategy	• Answering questions on investment analyses
• Creating a stronger capital allocation framework for the firm	• Reviewing junior team members' work
• Engaging with investors	• Managing the processes leading up to board meetings, investor meetings, and quarterly business reviews
• Repositioning the finance function to be strategic partners to other business units	• Going to internal meetings and joining calls to stay in the loop
• Developing a succession plan for the CFO	

right level for my role and my goals?" and making an honest assessment of how he was actually spending his time compared to where he should be focusing his efforts was critical for Alex to realize he was blocked (though as we would soon find out, he wasn't the only one to see it).

As we debriefed his list, I asked Alex, "I'm curious. To what extent do you think you need to be doing all the things on the right side of the board and be in all these meetings that commandeer your schedule?"

"Believe me, Muriel, I wish I didn't need to! But seriously, if I wasn't, you can't imagine the hell that would break loose. *I need to be involved* at this level or else it's a hot mess."

"So you believe that you need to be involved in every task and detail or it's likely something will go wrong?"

Alex shrugged. "I know that's not *literally* true . . . but yeah, that's accurate."

There it was: the real issue that was blocking Alex from leading more strategically was not his lack of time. The real blocker was his belief that he had to be involved—because if he wasn't, there was a strong chance that things would go wrong. Alex had named his hidden blocker.

Signs You May Have This Hidden Blocker

What you may see and feel

You expect team members at all levels to keep you updated and in the loop, and become frustrated when they don't.

You want to review and weigh in on deliverables and action items before they are completed.

You laser in on the details, even when they're not in your area or they're someone else's responsibility.

You feel resentment that so much is on your plate and you have no time.

What others may see and feel

You have the reputation of being a micromanager.

You take the lead in meetings even when others are supposed to.

You accept most meeting requests, even if you're already overcommitted.

You insist on being included on every email.

You won't let things proceed or won't sign off on deliverables until you weigh in.

You are hard to get a hold of because you're so busy.

Alex Unpacks His Hidden Blocker

After our kickoff meeting, I conducted feedback interviews with Alex's team members, peers, and boss to get additional context. Here's some of what I heard about Alex's strengths:

- "He's very analytical. He's hands-on and detail-oriented."

- "He's a huge asset to the firm. He's super honest and hustles. He's whip-smart and understands his space. He's creative in trying to find outcomes that work."

- "Alex is always willing to roll up his sleeves and doesn't shy away from the details."

- "He will take things and run with them. He has a lot of initiative."

But Alex's colleagues also made it clear that when overdone, some of his strengths were actually limiting his ability to add greater value as a CFO and member of the senior leadership team:

- "He takes on too much and doesn't delegate, which means he can become a bottleneck and weak on follow-through. He needs to check himself to make sure he's not feeling like he's the only one who can work on certain things and to get the help he needs from his team."

- "He has to discern where he can truly add value. He sometimes has a tough time prioritizing and ends up getting involved in things he doesn't really need to. He should be focusing on high-impact things that only a CFO can do."

- "He can get involved at a very detailed level and makes team members feel like they can't make decisions and that everything is questioned, which can be demoralizing. He needs to dial back on the micromanaging and allow his team space to grow."

- "His comfort zone is in the deeper execution of things instead of the higher-level things like external relationships. It can feel like he holds on to the execution so he actually owns something, but it keeps him at a tactical versus a strategic level, which is where we need him."

Alex was taken aback. "Wow, I know I have my hands in a lot of things, but micromanager? Bottleneck? Lack of focus? That's hard to hear. Especially when all I'm trying to do is make sure things stay on course. I'm not sure what people want from me. I get pulled into everything, and then they complain that I'm too much in the details and not focused on the important things. If people did what they were supposed to, I wouldn't need to be so involved."

Alex's defensiveness was a natural reaction. The negative feedback had caught him by surprise, especially when he felt he was going the extra mile to keep everything on track.

"Listen, I get it," I said, "but here's the thing. We need to look at the *impact* of your actions. Your intentions are one thing, but how your decisions and actions impact your colleagues and the goals you set for yourself is a different story."

When Alex and I dug further into the effects of his tendency to be overinvolved, there was plenty of evidence that his hidden blocker wasn't doing him any favors. In addition to limiting his bandwidth to work on strategic issues and leaving him feeling increasingly frustrated and unfulfilled, he noticed he was often curt with people because he felt like he was dealing with too much at once. Not only was he not winning any friends or allies, but he was also starting to get a reputation for being difficult to work with.

His team was also struggling. One star team member was viewed as a possible successor. However, she was becoming discouraged by Alex's desire to tag-team on everything rather than letting her run with some things on her own. She wasn't learning or gaining the experience and skills she needed to advance and was becoming a flight risk as a result. Alex's boss was also questioning whether Alex was doing enough to develop his people, as he wasn't seeing them confidently take the lead without Alex's involvement.

After hearing this, Alex admitted he wasn't having the impact he wanted, nor was this how he wanted to come off. He wanted to be more strategic, more elevated, not so much in the weeds. But he still wasn't convinced that he didn't need to be as involved as he was and came back with several examples of how his interventions had re-sulted in a good outcome.

I could hear his frustration. "I understand that being hyper-involved has worked well in the past," I said. "But you also just told me that the way you're currently acting is not how you want to show up. So how does justifying and defending the belief that's blocking you help?"

Alex winced. "Ouch. OK, let me own it, then."

"What does that mean to you?" I asked.

"It means saying, 'Yup, I do think I need to be involved in every-thing and I'm attending all these meetings I don't need to.' I can take the responsibility that it makes my team feel deflated and slows things down and can feel like micromanaging. And I guess owning it means I don't blame others for what's happening."

"Owning what's blocking you and seeing it for what it is is half the battle," I said. "Most folks can't even get there, let alone do something to change their behavior. So, kudos to you. The key is understanding why you hold on to this belief so that the next time you get stuck in it, it doesn't stay hidden, and you can course correct."

Alex's defensiveness was perfectly natural—well-established pat-terns can be hard to let go—and it gave us an opportunity to explore why this blocker had such a powerful grip on him. Without that understanding, it would just remain in his way.

Alex shared his fear that if he pulled back, "everything" would get off track, and then he would be the one "left to clean up the mess."

"What you're telling me," I said, "is that if you're not involved, things can't get done in the right way, and then you're left to fix it?"

"Exactly."

"And this happens in everything, every time? And you are the only person who can handle all of these situations in the right way?"

Alex paused. "OK, so now I sound very full of myself. I didn't mean it that way. We've got some folks who can step in."

"OK, if they've got their own mandate and they're capable of ful-filling it, and you have yours, what do you think you really need to be involved in?" I asked.

"That's a great question," he said, "because to be honest, I guess I don't know. I thought I knew. But this whole process clearly tells me I got it wrong. I haven't really been intentional about what I should or shouldn't be involved in because I've been in damage-control mode."

"And what's the damage you're trying to control, exactly?"

"Hmm, half the time I don't even know," Alex said. "All I know is I don't want anything to go wrong, so I do all I can to make sure it doesn't. That's why I get involved, even when I'm not asked to or I'm not needed there. I mean, now that I say all this out loud, it sounds pretty illogical."

"There's nothing illogical about it," I said. "In fact, I think you've just come up with a great insight. But let me ask you this—in what way has damage-control mode helped you?"

"It keeps stuff from blowing up."

"OK, let me play back what I'm hearing you say. You believe everything has the potential to blow up, so you get super involved to make sure nothing goes wrong . . . and you also think you're the only one who's capable enough to prevent these catastrophes. Sound accurate?"

"Well, it sounds pretty awful. . . . But yeah, deep down I think that's true."

Alex and I spent the rest of our conversation examining some of these assumptions. Did *everything* really have equal blow-up potential? Did he really have to do damage control for all things? Were there others who were just as capable—and even if not, could they become capable if he gave them space to try? No, no, and yes.

"Look, I think you've accomplished a ton by being highly involved," I said. "But you're so tied to your role as the damage controller that it's holding you back from creating value in areas where only *you* can as the CFO. It's preventing you from doing the very thing you came here to do."

Alex was starting to move from not just naming and accepting his blocker but to exploring its deeper layers so he could address what was happening at the core. I knew that Alex had been a straight-A student much of his life, he'd attended prestigious schools, and he'd advanced to the C-suite in an industry where it was incredibly difficult to do so. I reminded him of how much success he'd enjoyed already, and I asked what he thought contributed to it.

"I've just always made sure to have all my bases covered," he said. "I'm that guy on the field who plays his position really well and also knows what every other player is supposed to do and steps in when it seems like they can't."

That was another piece to our puzzle: Alex attributed much of his success to his ability to stay on top of everything. To be, in other words, overly involved.

Alex also shared that he regretted times when he could have intervened to keep things from going wrong and hadn't. He remembered how, early in his career, he had gotten chewed out by a managing director in front of his peers because an intern under his supervision incorrectly color-coded a spreadsheet. "You'd better double-proof, triple-proof, and quadruple-proof everything, Alex!" the director had yelled, leaving Alex deeply embarrassed and doubting his capabilities, all because of a small mistake he hadn't even made. He took a major hit that day and, without knowing it, made a deal with himself that he'd never let something go wrong on his watch again. As a result of this and other such experiences, Alex had developed the habit of rescuing, often before rescuing was needed. While he trusted himself to deliver on expectations, he was unwilling to take the risk of letting others try and possibly fail.

The Roots of This Hidden Blocker

We all have good reasons why our hidden blockers emerged in the first place. They never come out of thin air. As we learned in chapter 1, they serve a purpose. The issue is when the purpose they were initially meant to serve runs counter to what we're trying to accomplish now.

Potential Costs of This Hidden Blocker

Inability to fulfill your mandate: Getting overly involved in others' work means leaders may underdeliver in areas where only they can add value—things like setting a vision, driving strategy, and influencing across the organization.

Inability to scale: Being involved at so many levels and in so many things makes it impossible to keep up and undermines the opportunity to demonstrate leadership skills. When this happens, it's easy to be overlooked for opportunities to move up or take on more.

Lack of responsiveness: Being overcommitted and unavailable means teams, clients, customers, or other stakeholders may not receive timely responses.

Teams suffer: When leaders are overly involved in others' work, it deprives team members of the opportunity to own anything or to learn, grow, and develop new skills, and some end up leaving.

Left out of the loop: Frustrated and slowed down by their need to weigh in on everything, some colleagues, especially peers, choose to circumvent leaders as part of the process, resulting in the very thing these leaders are trying to avoid—not being involved.

What's the source of the "I need to be involved" hidden blocker? Everyone will have their own origin story, but it's generally a protection mechanism rooted in the universal need to feel safe. Alex's past experiences had taught him that when things go wrong (for example, a spreadsheet mistake), the world can feel unsafe (his boss flies off the handle). Exerting control was Alex's way of keeping things safe. *If I'm vigilant enough*, the thinking goes, *nothing will go wrong, and I can't be called out or hindered.*

What I've seen in my work with clients who have this hidden blocker is that it's really about protecting themselves from an underlying fear that if something goes wrong, they won't be able to handle the aftermath. This lack of confidence in their ability to deal with "stuff blowing up," as Alex put it, drives them to do everything they can to make sure that nothing ever goes wrong. The difficulty, frustration, and disappointment they imagine experiencing if things fall apart is too much to take. It's no surprise that Alex and many other leaders have this fear because, on the one hand, they've been rewarded, often lavishly, for rolling up their sleeves and taking care of things, and on the other, they've sometimes been punished when things fall through the cracks—even small things like a color-coding error by an intern.

I can relate. Like Alex, I was very adept at keeping lots of balls in the air in my professional life. In fact, others openly wondered how I did so much and made it look easy. My breaking point came when I took on an additional job while leading my rapidly growing business— that of being a mother. When my twins were born, I believed I could approach my expanded responsibilities in the same way I had tackled everything else: I'd involve myself in every detail to ensure it was all under control.

But the scope of my responsibilities at home and at work had expanded dramatically, and I failed to realize that meant I needed to think and act differently. It's a mistake many leaders make when they're asked to scale up, take on an additional division, go from managing a small team to a big one, or manage other managers for the first time. The great irony was that I was coaching leaders about how to scale when their roles expanded yet not heeding my own advice. Little did I realize that becoming a mom would be the ultimate test of my capacity for trying to be involved in everything.

My aspiration was to be a present, conscious parent. In reality, my hidden blocker had me obsessed with every little detail down to creating an Excel spreadsheet that documented when the twins slept, ate, pooped, smiled, or made sounds. I wanted a full report from our childcare provider, Veronica, every time I came home, and got upset if she didn't text me with real-time updates or if she changed the kids' schedule without checking with me. Needless to say, I wasn't winning any favorite-person trophies from the people who were there to support me as I onboarded into motherhood. And the constant vigilance made the exhaustion I was facing as a new parent worse.

Veronica was the one who eventually helped me uncover the hidden blocker that had me in its clutches. One day, I was complaining that no one was filling out my spreadsheet. Veronica, in her gentle voice, said, "You know, people believe they can control everything and somehow it will keep bad things from happening. Kids will teach you that's not the case." In her wisdom, Veronica had pinpointed that I was under the illusion that being involved in everything would keep unwanted things from happening—that if I could control every little detail about their lives, my kids wouldn't get sick, fall, or encounter obstacles in life.

My hidden blocker showed up big time when I became a parent, but this belief sprouted long before my kids were born. Growing up, I was often sick with chronic bronchial issues. When I wasn't, my parents were on a constant quest to prevent me from falling ill again, which meant not being able to play with other kids, go outside, or participate in everyday activities. While it protected me, that script of "do everything you can to avoid getting sick" eventually became "do everything you can so that nothing goes wrong." As a new parent I was in the weeds, hoping that if I was deeply involved in all aspects of my newborns' care, I could stop anything bad from happening to them. My need to be overinvolved, to control every little detail, didn't originate when I became a mom, but it was the wake-up call that enabled me to see how this limiting belief had permeated many aspects of my personal and professional life. It had been with me for a long time.

Can you relate? A lot of people can. The need to feel in control runs deep and goes back to our innate drive to feel safe. We have a natural aversion to uncertainty because it threatens our sense of control, and studies show that we actually prefer knowing that something bad will happen rather than being unable to predict or control what could happen next.[2] Here are some common experiences that can lead people to develop the hidden blocker "I need to be involved":

- You faced negative consequences or were blamed when something went wrong.

- You saw someone else get penalized when something went wrong.

- You observed and learned this behavior from an authority figure in your life, such as a parent, teacher, or boss.

- Your life experiences taught you that you have to cover all your bases or else there will be a price to pay.

When Alex saw that his hidden blocker had not emerged out of nowhere but had been forming for some time, he realized that he'd also let it take over. The question now was whether he'd let a different, supportive belief lead him.

Alex Unblocks from His Hidden Blocker

Alex wanted to step up to the strategic parts of his role and the challenges associated with leading more people. But he couldn't lead effectively at scale as long as he focused on being the damage controller. Until he shifted his belief to align with his ideal outcome, nothing was going to change. To choose a different belief that would support his desire to lead more strategically, he had to be clear about what he wanted.

"Alex," I said, "imagine that six months from now, you are leading more strategically. What would that look like?"

"I'd be at the table with senior members of the firm discussing strategic issues," he said. "I would have a clearly articulated perspective on how we can gain a competitive advantage based on innovative financial approaches. I'd have the headspace to actually think about these things. I would also be way more externally focused than I am now by building relationships with key folks at the banks we deal with. I think in order to do all of that, my team would have to step up so that I can step up."

"So your team determines whether you can step up to being more strategic?"

"Ah, no. I need to flip that—I need to step up if I want my team to step up."

"Exactly. You see how that little nuance changes things? Focus on what *you* can do. What do you need to do to be able to make that six-month vision a reality?"

"I'd need to delegate a heck of a lot more than I do now," he said. "I definitely need to let go of being in every meeting and focus on the ones where my presence makes a difference. And I need to pull back from all the little details because there are just too many at this point and it's becoming impossible to keep up. Like the spreadsheets. I'm a CFO, not an analyst, and I need to keep reminding myself of that."

We spent some time further defining and zeroing in on the difference in leadership impact Alex wanted to make. Table 3-2 outlines what he came up with.

I then asked Alex what would need to change for him to be the leader on the right side of the table.

"I need to let go of the notion that 'I need to be involved in everything,' because obviously that is not the way I add value as a CFO," he said. "The belief that would work better for me is, 'I need to mainly be involved where I add the most value as CFO.' If that guides me, I have a way better chance of being the strategic leader I thought I'd be when I took this job."

By understanding what he wanted his future to look like, Alex was able to articulate the belief that would get him there and move away from the one that was holding him back.

With a new belief to drive him, Alex was ready for the final step in the Blocked to Unblocked Roadmap: to define and commit to tak-

TABLE 3-2

Alex's leadership impact: Current state versus desired state

My current leadership impact	My desired leadership impact
Transactional CFO who is deep in the weeds and very hands-on with day-to-day activities of his function	Strategic CFO who is able to zoom in and zoom out as needed while focusing on creating and driving value for the firm

ing actions that were aligned with his ideal future. If he had moved to action without reframing his hidden blocker, change would have been short-lived. His unblocked belief was his new anchor and helped him clearly describe how to lead moving forward. When I asked Alex to pull together a six-month action plan based on his commitment "to mainly be involved where I add the most value as CFO," he came up with two lists: what he should start doing—and what he should stop doing (see table 3-3).

Over the course of our coaching, Alex went from being blocked by his belief that he needed to be involved in all the details to making a much more significant impact as CFO. By shifting his perspective to "I need to mainly be involved where I add the most value as CFO," he refocused his attention to strategy formulation, cultivating external relationships, and developing his team. Did that mean he did nothing other than those objectives? No. But he made sure those three areas were priorities in terms of where he spent his time and energy.

By moving past his hidden blocker, Alex was able to refocus his actions on being less transactional and more strategic and role-appropriate. His team reported higher engagement as they felt more ownership over their work. The potential successor who had been a flight risk was empowered to lead more of the work without Alex constantly by her side. As a result, she gained more visibility and earned a promotion. The senior partners recognized Alex's efforts to drive more strategic discussions and invited him to share more of his perspective on the firm's future. And Alex shared with me

TABLE 3-3

Alex's six-month action plan to lead as a strategic CFO

Start doing	Stop doing
• Define overall finance framework approach for the firm	• Project-manage finance workstreams
• Lead and participate in meetings requiring CFO-level input	• Attend noncritical meetings to stay informed and/or keep an eye on team members
• Develop strategic perspective on financing options in support of overall firm growth goals	• Focus on lower-level activities such as proofreading, formatting, work planning
• Delegate noncritical meetings, analytical work, and cross-functional junior-level meetings to team members	• Liaise between team and other units in the firm on all things
• Identify and focus on cultivating high-value external relationships	

that although his overall workload had not decreased, he felt more fulfilled by his work and less stressed. He felt less scattered and frustrated and was able to empower the members of his team, providing more direction and opportunities for them to grow and shine, so they were less frustrated too. Over time, Alex's new approach helped him to disentangle himself from the day-to-day details, contribute more strategic value to his firm, and build a high-performing team that delivered results and showcased Alex's best qualities as a leader.

Coach Yourself

It can be so tempting to get overly involved because, as we saw with Alex, it can feel like you're doing the right thing by trying to ensure everything stays on course. Despite your best intentions, however, this hidden blocker can keep you too busy and scattered, and keep teams from owning their roles and growing.

Do you share Alex's hidden blocker of "I need to be involved"? To start shifting your mindset and reduce unnecessary involvement, begin by identifying how this specific belief shows up for you and naming it. Then, take your belief and reframe it in a way that supports a healthier balance, so you're engaged only where you add the most value.

From Blocked

- I need to be involved.

- I have to sweat all the details.

- I have to know what's happening.

- I need to be directly involved for things to go smoothly.

- I need to be in the loop on everything to ensure things go well.

- If I don't keep everyone on track, things won't get done.

To Unblocked

- I need to focus my involvement where I add the most value.

- I can do anything, but I can't do everything.

- The same level of involvement is not required for everything.

- I should get involved according to the level of opportunity and risk at hand.

- My level of involvement is determined by the unique value I bring to a situation.

- I don't need to oversee everything to contribute meaningfully.

To Action

- *Delegate tasks.* Assign responsibilities, building confidence in others and allowing you to focus on key areas.

- *Set clear priorities.* Identify which areas need your involvement and which can be managed by others.

- *Schedule regular check-ins instead of constant oversight.*
  Establish a structure for periodic updates rather than close
  monitoring.

- *Reflect on successes achieved without your involvement.*
  Remind yourself of positive outcomes, reinforcing trust and
  reducing the need for control. Recognize others' contributions
  to foster mutual rapport.

Chapter 4

I Need It Done Now

*The day will never arrive when you finally have
everything under control.*

—OLIVER BURKEMAN

Ann was the vice president of marketing at her company. Hired right
out of college, she'd risen from marketing associate to manager and
director positions, and then to her current role after being promoted
two years ago. As VP, she oversaw a large team responsible for the
branding of the company. Several directors reported to her, each of
whom supervised their own team.

I had previously coached Ann when she was a director and part of
a high-potential leadership development program. She was very well-
regarded in the organization and deemed an approachable leader
who built strong relationships throughout the company, from those
down the ranks to her peers to those more senior than her. Given her
uncanny ability to engage and motivate everyone and her extensive institutional knowledge, she was seen as a culture carrier. Many com-
mented in her 360-degree feedback that she always went the extra
mile. The head of talent management had shared with me back then
that Ann was seen as a potential successor to the chief marketing

officer and that her next role as VP would be the preparation ground
for that. Sure enough, within a few months of completing the leadership
development program, Ann was promoted to VP and was reporting
to the longtime chief marketing officer, Noah.

Now, two years later, I got an email from Ann asking if she could
run something by me. It's not out of the norm for my clients to keep in
touch, and I looked forward to catching up with her. We scheduled a
Zoom meeting and, after exchanging a few pleasantries, got into it.

"So, how's the VP gig going?" I asked.

"It's been really, really busy," she said. "There's so much to
be done, but it's all important stuff that's going to change the way
we're positioned in the marketplace. My team is great. They're creative and energetic. And Noah's been so supportive—he's involved
me in major decisions and trusts me to get the job done and is super
understanding with all the stuff happening outside of work."

"Oh, what's going on there?"

"You know, just life. My mom's been sick—she was diagnosed
with breast cancer again. But she's in treatment, and I help out when-
ever I can, and we're hoping for the best. And my daughter is thir-
teen now—can you believe it? I keep wanting to volunteer at her
school, but you know how it goes. I can't seem to find the time. And
she's acting up a bit . . . going through normal teen angst, I guess."

"How are you holding up through all this?" I asked.

"I'm a bit tired, but what else is new? But this brings me to what I
wanted to run by you. Noah said something the other day and I
wasn't sure how to take it. He said he feels like I'm either going to
burn myself out or burn the team out, or both, if I don't slow down.
It kind of caught me off guard; I actually wasn't sure if he was joking.
Because it's not like *he* doesn't run hard. So I just laughed it off. But
a few days later, my HR business partner shared the results of our
latest employee engagement survey with me, and now I wonder if
Noah's comment had to do with that. We did better than the rest of
the company in team dynamics and understanding the company's vision, but there are other areas where we actually scored close to the

lowest—key areas like work-life balance/well-being, strategic direction, and priority setting."

"What do you make of those results?" I asked.

"To be honest, I'm not sure," Ann said. "On the one hand, people say they're excited about the work and energized by each other and the recognition they get. On the other hand, they say they're unclear about priorities and overworked. I know we work hard, but I didn't think anyone felt like they were doing too much. What worries me most is that we've indexed lower in those areas since I took over. Noah and the rest of the executive leadership team take these employee engagement scores seriously. They're part of our overall performance assessment. So if I have any shot of being the next chief marketing officer, I can't afford for this trend to continue. But I also can't deliver results by letting everyone have a three-day workweek. I could use some help figuring out what to do."

Ann Uncovers Her Hidden Blocker

A few weeks after my catch-up call with Ann, we kicked off our second round of coaching. Top priority was getting a sense of what was behind Noah's comment about burnout, as well as the team's declining survey scores.

With Jen's permission, I sat down with her team leaders to learn more about what was happening and what part, if any, they felt Ann played in it. It quickly became apparent that they all very much liked Ann. Many of them knew her well given her long tenure at the company, and they shared how excited they were when she was named the new VP. One of her directors summed up the positive thinking about Ann well: "She's got that rare 'it' factor," he said. "She's energetic and approachable and she's really invested in what we're doing. Her enthusiasm is genuine, and it makes everyone want to work with her. And at the same time, she really *delivers*. I don't know one person who doesn't like being around her."

Given the team members' high regard for Ann, I could see it was difficult for them to be critical of her. They wanted to see Ann succeed, and they knew her heart was in the right place. But the impact she was making was a different story, and one they feared was unsustainable for the team and for her. Here's some of what they shared with me, which shed light on the declining scores as well as Noah's comment:

- "She goes full speed on every action item that comes up and treats everything with equal importance. This is great for getting the ball rolling but detrimental in terms of priorities. It ends up feeling very reactionary. . . . She makes decisions based on whatever got to her last, instead of with an end goal in mind."

- "She brings an enviable amount of energy and drive but needs to have a more strategic, overall focus. It's unclear where her priorities are because she wants to do it all—and all at once. It often feels like we're playing 'whack a mole' and addressing whatever the most recent issue is. Priorities shift constantly."

- "She's aggressive with timelines but has unrealistic expectations. Her enthusiasm doesn't match the reality of where we are as a team."

- "She says work-life balance is important, but she doesn't walk the talk. She messages at all hours, and she's in the office almost every weekend. It's become a thing that if you want to catch up with Ann, come in on Sunday."

- "I'm concerned about her well-being. She's super productive and gets results but at what cost? Even when she was out for a few days with her mom, who's sick, she logged on to Zoom calls and the emails never stopped. People are talking about how work is starting to take a toll on her. Lately she's been sharp with us, which is very unlike her."

While it would be uncomfortable for them, the team felt it was important to deliver this feedback to Ann themselves. I would be there to help facilitate.

I prepared Ann for the feedback meeting, emphasizing that her role was to do only one thing: listen.

"You've got to give them your undivided attention," I said. "That means no multitasking. No hijacking the conversation with whatever fire drill is happening. None of that. It takes a lot of courage for your team to have this conversation."

"OK, now I'm super curious and scared at the same time, so let's just get this done and over with!"

On the day of the meeting, I could see she was nervous. As we walked to the conference room, I gave her one last reminder that everyone had her back and they were sharing their thoughts because they believed in her and wanted to see her succeed. She gave me a quick nod, and as soon as she was through the door, she was in driving mode. Ann kicked off the conversation by thanking everyone for their participation and then acknowledged that it may feel uncomfortable or awkward to offer her feedback face-to-face, but she genuinely welcomed it and hoped it was something they could continue in the future. She shared that the most recent employee data had surprised her, and she wanted to get to the underpinnings of it so they could address whatever issues were at hand. Then she uncapped her pen and got ready to take notes.

"Cassie, why don't you start?" Ann said to the team member sitting immediately to her right. "Then we'll just go around the table clockwise and maybe everyone can name their biggest concerns."

Cassie, looking a bit startled by the cold call, recovered quickly. "Well, the main thing I take away from the survey results is that the marketing group is feeling overworked and burned out," she said. "It basically confirms what I'm observing on my team, and I've got to say I'm feeling it too, like I never have before at this company. There's a number of things that contribute to this, but to me the largest one is we don't have focus—we're trying to do everything all at once. And, Ann, you know you and I go way back and I'm your biggest cheerleader, but when you're in firefighting mode, we're in firefighting mode. It trickles down. You bring such incredible energy and passion to the work, and I love that. But a lot of times that energy turns into doing too much and working too many hours. Our folks just can't operate like this all the time."

"Wow. Thank you so much for sharing that," Ann said. "I really appreciate the honesty. So, what can I do about this? I'm thinking I can have a meeting with each of your teams. And maybe we can implement something where everyone gets an extra day off. Would that help?"

It was time for me to gently weigh in.

"Ann, if I may, why don't we wait until everyone has shared their thoughts before you respond. I don't know if you see what's happening here, but your propensity to jump to action quickly like you just did is what's causing some of what you're about to hear. So if you're good with it, let's finish going around the table."

"Yes, let's continue," Ann said, "and I promise I'll hold off on commenting." She drew pinched fingers across her lips to indicate she'd remain silent.

One by one, each direct report shared their observations, while Ann took it all in. They all reflected the same themes: feeling overworked, constant fire drills, shifting priorities, being "on" all the time, duplicated efforts, and a sense of urgency with everything—all of which felt like a direct result of Ann's management approach.

"What concerns me the most," said the last person, "is we're now all taking on a 'ready, shoot, aim' approach just to keep up, and it's becoming our overall team culture. Is that what we really want? If so, we should expect the survey scores to stay on a downward trend, and worse, I think we could end up losing some of our most talented people."

When the last person finished, I looked over at Ann, who was visibly eager to respond.

"So, Ann," I said, "what are your thoughts? Let's start with how you feel about what you heard, but let's not jump to what you want to do about it just yet."

Ann turned to her team. "OK, so first off, let me just say thank you. I don't take it lightly what you've done just now. Being super candid with me about your concerns is no small feat for anyone. I'm proud that we've built a team where you can do that.

"And if I'm being honest, I admit this is a lot to take in. I know we work hard, but I didn't realize the extent to which it was impacting everyone. When I took over the VP role, what I looked forward to most was building a team and a place to work that people were excited about. Not just because of what we're working on but also because of the culture. It's disappointing to hear the team feels the way it does. So look, I know we're already running over our meeting time, and I don't want to hold you up. Let me figure out what we can do about this and circle back soon."

The meeting adjourned.

"Well, *that* was a shit show!" Ann said as soon as the last person left. "I wasn't expecting things to be *this* bad. I think I know what I need to do, though. I've already jotted down some action items and—"

"Whoa, whoa, whoa," I said, putting my hands in a time-out position. "Let's pause for a sec. Do you see what's happening?"

"What do you mean? I see myself facing all this criticism head-on and trying to do something about it." she said. "Which is not easy, I might add."

"No, it's not," I said. "But I mean before that. Let's do a quick playback. You literally just heard your team say the issue is too many fire drills and too much speed to react to whatever pops up, yet the first thing you do coming out of that conversation is launch another self-imposed fire drill. What happened between what you heard and now?"

Ann threw up her hands. "I don't know! I heard their concerns. And now *I just need to do something about it* so we can move on."

Signs You May Have This Hidden Blocker

What you may see and feel

You worry you're never doing enough, and you feel guilty when you're not being productive.

You are always in pursuit of finishing everything on your to-do list, even when that list is never-ending.

Work and tasks are constantly on your mind, even when you're not at work.

You put off activities such as connecting with friends and family, going to the doctor, exercising, or taking time off because you feel you don't have the time and have too much to do.

You focus on what hasn't been done, rather than on what has.

"And you need to do it right away?"

"Well, sure," she said. "After hearing that from your team, wouldn't it kick in to do something immediately?"

"OK, that thing that kicks in and tells you 'do something immediately,'" I said. "That's a thought. A thought you probably didn't even know was there. But it's driving you to act quickly. And I'm going to bet this isn't the first and only time this thought kicks in, or is it?"

Ann paused. "It isn't," she said. "It's like I've got this inner Arnold Schwarzenegger constantly yelling, 'Do it! Do it now!'" We both laughed, and Ann continued. "Who wants Arnie yelling at them all the time? Not my team, that's for sure. And I don't want that either."

Ann realized that her Arnie-inflected command not only was affecting how she approached her work and interacted with her team, but had led to the very situation her team was now in, along with those decreasing engagement scores.

You prefer to engage in activities with a clear outcome or closure.

You accept that a heavy workload and putting in long hours are just part of the job.

What others may see and feel

You have a reputation for being relentless, tireless, extremely driven, and/or a taskmaster.

You move fast and get a lot done.

You check in frequently with others to make sure they're on task and expect a response right away.

You approach everything as highly urgent.

You pressure others to work at the same speed and urgency as you do.

Ann Unpacks Her Hidden Blocker

At our next coaching session, I brought Ann a small gift: an Arnold Schwarzenegger bobblehead doll. When she opened up the package, she laughed out loud.

"This is awesome!" she exclaimed. "I've gotta tell you, I've been noticing my inner Arnie ever since we last met. I feel myself wanting to say, 'Do it now!' and I've actually said it a few times, even if not in those exact words. It was so much easier when I didn't know how the team felt. Now I don't know what to do with all that . . . or if I even can do something about it."

That wasn't because Ann was unwilling. It was because she and her team were facing down several nonnegotiables at once.

"We have aggressive revenue goals, we're relaunching our brand campaign, and our marketing analytics division lacks serious capabilities, so we need to beef that up, like yesterday," she said.

"I understand everybody wants to slow down. But we can't. Not right now."

"When can you?"

"In a few months, once we get through the brand campaign re-launch. But until then, it's just not possible."

"Do you ever let up?" I asked.

"What do you mean?"

"In the past two years, has there been any breathing room for you and your team?"

"No, not really," she said. "This has been the normal state of affairs for this team for the past few years—and for me, forever."

"Exactly. The reality is there's been no letting up. There always seems to be something to get in the way of the break everyone needs. So what makes you think it's going to be different this time?"

"Look, I know, I know," Ann said. "But what am I supposed to do? Let us fall behind? Am I wrong for wanting us to be successful?"

"Well, it all depends. How are you defining success? Because until now, it sounds like success for you has meant getting things done—as in everything, very quickly. The question is, are you good with the trade-offs you're making for your team—and you for that matter—in order to get things done? Because whether you're aware of it or not, you're choosing to make trade-offs that are leading your team to burn out for the sake of getting everything done."

Ann leaned back in her chair and let out a big sigh. "Of course that's not what I intended, or what I want for anyone," she said. "I just hate the feeling of not being able to do it all. But I can see that's my thing and not theirs, and they're paying the consequences."

"What about you?"

"Oh, I definitely pay too. I can't remember the last time I didn't work on a weekend. I can't even sneak in a workout. And let's not even talk about a real vacation when I'm not on my laptop half the time."

Many leaders who operate with the belief that they must get all their tasks done before they allow themselves to do anything other than work end up—guess what—never getting around to doing anything other than working. The constant deferral can affect anything from daily habits to overarching goals: "If I can get through all these items, then I'll go to the gym." "If I can make partner by next year, then I'll allow myself a vacation." "If I hustle now and retire early, then I'll take that class/write my book/start the business I've always wanted to."

It applies to goals at work as well. I've heard from many leaders who really want to do more for their team members, such as plan an offsite retreat or provide more mentoring, but never get around to it because they can't find their way to the end of their to-do list. Whatever that end goal is, there are a million and one to-dos that *must* be completed before they will allow themselves a break or go after something they really want.

Ironically, these results-driven leaders are also missing out on one of the most effective means for being more productive and improving performance, for themselves and their teams: taking breaks. Work recovery, or the practice of regularly detaching from work in order to unwind and recover from work-related stress, leads to better sleep, more energy, higher engagement, and better performance. And one need not save up for a vacation or a long weekend to enjoy the benefits of work recovery: research has found that short microbreaks throughout the day, such as taking a walk outside, stretching, having a social chat, or doing a mindfulness activity such as deep breathing or meditation, deliver the same stress-relieving, performance-enhancing effects.[1] Leaders need to engage in work recovery for their own benefit as well as to model the practice for their teams, and build taking breaks into the culture.

"What do you think *really* needs to change to get you and your team the breather you all need?" I asked Ann.

"I guess it starts with me," she said. "The hard part about this is I don't know how else to be and whether it's possible to get results without thinking this way. At this point in my life, can I really change? I get things done; I'm a driver. Can I change that?"

"There's a difference between who you truly are and the habitual thought patterns and behaviors you've picked up because they served you well at certain points in time," I said. "Your ability to drive and get things done is hugely helpful. But is it necessary and appropriate at all times?"

I gave Ann a rather unusual assignment at the end of our coaching meeting. We were heading into the weekend, and I asked her to commit to taking sixty minutes on Saturday or Sunday to sit on her couch and do nothing. This exercise is an adaptation from the book *Four Thousand Weeks: Time Management for Mortals*, by Oliver Burkeman, who borrowed it from Jennifer Roberts, an art history professor at Harvard University. Roberts requires her students to stare at a painting of their choice for *three* full hours, in the hope of teaching them "the lost art of patience." Burkeman describes it as a meditative exercise: "You're watching your own reactions and choosing not to let them dictate your behavior, which would be to get up and leave and do something that kept you busier."[2] But knowing that Ann (like many of my coaching clients) would balk at the word *meditation*, I opted for a more palatable, though not easier, assignment: one hour of doing nothing.

"Do nothing!" Ann exclaimed. "What does that even *mean*? Can I sleep, read a book, watch a show?"

"It means do nothing," I said. "Just sit there. And see what happens. Jot your thoughts down when you're *finished* with your sixty minutes—but not before."

"I'll try," Ann said.

At our next meeting, I asked Ann how her assignment went.

"It was torture!" she said. "First of all, I sat on the couch, and within five minutes, my husband walked by and was like, 'What are you doing?' and when I said, 'Nothing,' he was like 'No, really. What are you doing?' and when I told him, he just laughed. He said I wouldn't last ten minutes."

"And did you?"

"I did!" she said. "You know I'm good with an assignment."

I asked her what she noticed during that time.

"At first I was really annoyed that I'd agreed to do this because I felt like there were so many other productive things I could be doing," she said. "All I could think about is all the things I had to do. Some that are already on my list and new ones that were popping up. And then I also felt really guilty just sitting there doing nothing. It was harder than I expected. It feels useless, like a waste of time."

"You're describing how you felt about the exercise," I said. "Can you tell me more about how you felt about *you* while doing nothing?"

"*I* felt useless. Like I had no idea how to be without having something to do, and then it made me feel anxious that I was probably letting someone down by just sitting there as the minutes dragged by."

"And who exactly were you letting down by sitting quietly for an hour on a Sunday?"

"My inner Arnie?" Ann responded and cracked a smile. "OK, yes, this all goes back to me again. I felt like I was letting myself down, but that was only because I wasn't engaged in actively doing anything. Even if nobody was waiting for me to deliver something on Sunday morning, I still felt on. Muriel, I get the point of the exercise, but with all due respect, I don't think it's realistic. I didn't get where I am by doing nothing."

"No offense taken," I said. "But let me make sure I'm understanding you. Inherent in what you're saying is that you got where you are by doing. Is that right?"

"Absolutely," said Ann. "I was never the smartest student or the most talented athlete. But one thing I knew how to do was outwork everyone. My senior year in college, my basketball team created the Hustle Award in my honor to recognize the player who could make things happen on and off the court. That's always been my thing. I hustle. And it's also the work ethic I was brought up with. Even as a kid, I'm the one everyone turned to to take care of things. Maybe because I'm the oldest of my siblings? I even remember my mom

Potential Costs of This Hidden Blocker

Exhaustion and eventual burnout: Leaders and team members who feel they need to be available and ready to respond at any moment suffer from unrelenting stress and overwork. Emotional, mental, and physical exhaustion can result from chronic overwork and insufficient rest and sleep, and unmanaged work-related stress leads to burnout.

Unclear priorities and decreased productivity: In this paradoxical outcome, productivity and performance can falter due to overwork and exhaustion, or because leaders have trouble identifying priority items that move the needle. Their strong bias to action leads them to treat everything with equal urgency, and every new task or problem must be dealt with ASAP. Team members are left scrambling to keep up, constantly shifting gears to address the latest mandate from the leader. Older action items can get lost in the shuffle as the leader quickly moves to whatever is in front of them.

saying to me, 'Get all your homework and chores done no matter what and make sure your sisters do too and then you can go out and play.' The work always came first above all else."

"And what did that do for you?"

"I mean, at the risk of sounding cocky, it differentiated me. It made me stand out from the pack, and I've moved up because of how productive I am. It's not lost on me that my ability to get things done has been a huge factor in my success. Being reliable, thorough, and super productive became my superpower. It's how I was able to get my MBA with honors while holding down a full-time job and being a new mom. I've always been able to crank through things. And I think in a weird way, it's kept me away from failure. I've probably always been a little afraid that if I didn't keep up and deliver, I wouldn't make the cut."

"So fast-forward to today, how does that play out for you now?"

Division between team members: Favoritism can easily set in as the leader with this hidden blocker consciously or unconsciously recognizes team members who have the same bias to action they do. This can also foster an overly competitive workplace culture where team members feel that if they unplug or let up, someone else will do more and get ahead or gain favor.

Loss of key team members: In an effort to distance themselves from their work-related stress, overworked team members are at risk for disengagement, increased absenteeism, and quiet quitting or actual quitting.

Harm to relationships outside of work: Leaders with this hidden blocker place higher priority on task completion than on people. This can have an impact on their personal relationships with partners, children, and friends as work takes precedence over connecting and spending time with loved ones outside of work.

"Well, just like it did in that 'do nothing' exercise. When I feel like I'm not doing anything, I feel useless. So if I overlap that with work, the same thing happens. I'm only as useful and successful as how many things I can get done."

"When does your to-do list end?"

"It doesn't. That's the issue. As much as I'm crossing off, I'm always adding on. I always feel like I can be doing more. So if I'm really honest with myself, I probably never truly feel successful because success is always out of reach. I'm never satisfied, and nothing is ever enough because the tasks keep coming and the job is never done."

"And that's not a good feeling, is it?"

"Not at all," Ann said. "And now I'm realizing my team probably feels the same way. Like I didn't realize how my 'superpower' could land differently when I have to get things done through other people. One thing's for sure—it doesn't help my team's morale."

The Roots of This Hidden Blocker

Several streams of influence can result in the belief that we need to constantly hustle to get things done (and the more, the better), but common among them is that somewhere along the way, these leaders learned to equate success and self-worth with productivity. Many were the schoolkids who turned in their homework early and the college students who requested syllabi ahead of the semester to get a jump on the reading. They were praised for their diligence, strong work ethic, and great results, and learned early on to attach their self-worth to what and how much they could accomplish. Some are natural overachievers who were intrinsically motivated to work hard and get a lot done; others experienced external pressure early in life to perform and achieve. Almost all have a strong fear of failure and are deeply motivated to avoid falling short and disappointing themselves and others.

This belief can develop or be reinforced later in life as well, as a result of working in environments that prize busyness, productivity, and being overscheduled. Workplaces characterized by "hustle culture," or environments where long hours and self-sacrifice are required to excel and be accepted, are the favored stomping grounds of this hidden blocker. Implicitly or explicitly, many organizations that glorify the grind encourage competitive overworking among team members, with winners being those who work the most and sleep the least. *Not* being overworked is a sign that you or your skills aren't in demand, or that you can't handle the pressure. It's no wonder that hustle culture is also known as burnout culture and has been linked with high stress, anxiety, depression, poor sleep quality, and even increased risk of cardiovascular disease and premature death.[3]

Leaders who believe they must get things done no matter the cost will often double down on their belief, pointing out—rightly—that they are valuable to their organizations precisely because they are so proactive and productive. The minute a task or a problem arises, they are on it, and there is no question they'll address it. But there is a difference between healthy productivity, where leaders and their teams complete tasks and accomplish goals in a timely manner without sacrificing their personal well-being, and toxic productivity, where leaders feel a strong or even obsessive urge to be "always on," regardless of the cost to their well-being, personal relationships, and the health of the team. The latter is exactly what was happening in Jen's situation. It had been evident to her team members for a while, and after some tough feedback, she could see it for herself. Leaders like Ann who are in the grip of toxic productivity are uncomfortable when they're idle, and even when they're busy, feel guilty for not doing more, faster. These leaders don't think the law of diminishing returns applies to them, refusing to believe that their overproductivity will eventually lead to *decreased* productivity and work quality, especially if exhaustion or illness catches up with them.

On other occasions, leaders throw themselves into overproductivity at work in order to avoid or distract themselves from something painful in other areas of their lives. A divorce, a health issue, a problem with a child, even loneliness . . . any challenge that leaves them feeling uncomfortable or out of control can lead them to focus intensely on getting things done and prioritizing work over everything else. What's a more absorbing and satisfying way to regain a sense of control than organizing our days into tidy to-do lists and checking off items one by one? And what's a more accepted and respected way to avoid tough situations than to devote yourself to work and get lots of things done?

At other times, the "something painful" comes from within. Plenty of leaders who are ruled by their to-do lists are unconsciously trying to ameliorate feelings of inadequacy or low self-esteem. Piling on more hours, more clients, more projects, more *busyness* is a way to demonstrate to themselves that they are valued and good at their jobs.

At heart, this belief is rooted in a desire to feel worthy, fulfilled, and in control—and honestly, who doesn't want all of that?

When I was a business school student, I vividly recall a conversation with some of my classmates late one night after dinner. We were talking about life, including our future plans and careers. I asked a question that I was likely asking myself but processed out loud for all my friends to hear: "How much is enough?"

The conversation came to an abrupt halt.

"What do you mean?" one of my friends finally asked.

"How will you know when you've worked enough and achieved enough and accumulated enough?" I said.

They all looked at me as though I were speaking a foreign language.

"What?" I said, with a nervous laugh. "Is that such a wild question to ask?"

"Well, kind of," another friend said. "I mean why would you ever *want* to feel like it's enough or put a limit on yourself that way?"

"Because I can't imagine feeling like a hamster running on a wheel the rest of my life," I said.

I've thought about that conversation a lot over the years, especially as I've worked with so many high-performing leaders like Ann who have a strong bias toward action and struggle with slowing down or taking a break. But for me, I saw red flags early on. Having watched many people close to me become workaholics and being very aware that I had all the traits to become one myself, I knew even as an MBA student that I didn't want to be seduced by the culture of "never enough," where no amount of work, money, or success is ever sufficient. It's not that the goalpost is always moving; it's that it's unattainable from the outset and yet we still hope we'll finally reach it. Part of the trouble, it seems, comes from those social expectations that we must keep striving, keep achieving, keep leveling up—that is, if we're not acquiring or doing more, we're not succeeding. And part of it comes from our natural tendency to become habituated to whatever new plateau we achieve, a phenomenon known as "hedonic adaptation."[4] The happiness we feel after a promotion or receiving positive feedback only lasts so long, and soon we feel compelled to achieve more to get back to our previous level of happiness.

As my career advanced and my responsibilities and tasks seemed to increase exponentially with every new leadership role, I knew I'd need to institute firm boundaries around my time and the amount of work I took on. Which is not to say that this old belief of always wanting to get everything done didn't crop up and drive my behavior from time to time. But being very familiar with what this hidden blocker looked like and the negative repercussions it could cause, from experiencing mental and physical exhaustion to missing out on time with family and friends to never getting around to pursuing my personal interests and passions, I wasn't willing to let this one take over. The most effective reframe for me was "I'll do my best within the time I have."

Ann Unblocks from Her Hidden Blocker

Ann had never placed a boundary on herself and was caught in a vicious cycle of her own doing. The more she believed that productivity was the key to her and her team's success, the more productive she became, and the more she tried to chase output as efficiently as possible. The more efficient she became in producing output, the more tasks she could add onto the plate. The more tasks she added onto the plate, the more productive she felt she needed to be. And so on. What Ann hadn't caught onto until now was that being too efficient can make us less effective by filling our time with more tasks. When I pointed this out to her, she acknowledged that she felt like she and her team were in the bucket-dumping business.

"When I was a kid, my family would go to the beach, and my sisters and I would dig a hole in the sand to build a castle," she explained. "But then water would start coming through the bottom of the hole. And we'd fill our buckets up with the water and run to the ocean and dump it out. But by the time we got back to the hole, it was filled with water again. So, we'd just try to do it faster, thinking we could beat the water, and the same thing would happen until it just tired us out and we'd give up. And my dad would say, 'Are y'all in the castle-building business or the bucket-dumping business?' In a way I feel like my team and I are more bucket dumpers than castle makers right now.'"

"And in your work scenario, what is the rising water that just keeps coming?"

"Tasks. Projects. Things to do."

"And what does the hole in the sand represent?"

"I guess it represents time. We have a limited amount of time to do all the things I want us to and also resources, like the number of people on my team. And just physical energy. I've been pushing my limits to achieve things for so long that it feels second nature to me, and I hate that there are limits on what we can do."

"As far as I know, you can't control time. You have twenty-four hours in a day. Nothing changes that."

"I know; I've tried!" she said with a laugh. "It's almost like trying to make the most out of all time we have is what makes things worth it to me, so I try to get as much done as possible during those twenty-four hours and I expect the same of my team. But the problem is, there's *always* too much to get done in the time we have. It's like I'm trying constantly to fill a month's worth of clothes into my little weekender carry-on. There's not enough organizing, shoving, or sitting on top of the suitcase that will fit it all in. It's either I need a bigger suitcase—which in the case of work, we don't have because we don't have more time or people—or bring fewer clothes, which basically means do less."

"Yes! And notice that 'do less' doesn't mean 'do nothing.' We don't need to go to that extreme. But what if you and the team do less? What would that require? Let's continue with the suitcase example."

"Well, if I had to travel for a few weeks and could only bring a small bag, I would have to make some choices. I'd have to think about where I'm going and figure out what I absolutely need—what are my non-negotiables. And then if there's room left, I'd see if there are some things on my 'nice to bring' list that I could fit in. And I'd have to make sure to leave a little room to bring back a gift for my daughter. So with work, I think it's the same. I really do try to fit everything in and then cram in more. We'll have to make some hard choices about what really matters, and that's going to require us to be clear about where we're going as a team. And also, just like the space for gifts, we need to leave a little slack in our work time for the surprises too."

"Beautiful. In order for you to lead with this approach, how will you need to think differently?"

"If success now means not only getting things done but also making sure my team is not burning out, I'm going to have to work on moving to the mantra 'We just need to get done what matters.' And that means accepting that it's OK that we have limits and that there are some things that I may want to do that are just not going to get done."

Over the next several months, the mantra "We just need to get done what matters" was adopted not only by Ann but also by her entire leadership team, who enthusiastically welcomed this new operating principle. It kicked off a series of discussions aimed at pruning the list of projects and initiatives and creating a filter to determine whether they took on something new or not. They got themselves into the practice of asking, "What's the worst that will happen if we wait before taking action on this, or if we don't do this at all?"

And most importantly, Ann had to role-model for the team that what they were doing and not doing was OK, which meant building her comfort level with *not* getting everything done. I shared with her the story I'd read of Father Simeon, a defense attorney turned monk, who, when asked what to do when you feel your work isn't finished at the end of your work time, responded, "You get over it." Rather than putting in marathon work sessions with no clear end, Father Simeon and his community work an assigned number of hours per day—and no more. Whatever is not done at the end of that day is simply left for the next. It's "a deeply humane approach to work," observes author Jonathan Malesic, that allows the monks to leave work behind "so they can get on with something much more important to them."[5]

To stay on track with this newfound approach, Ann pulled together a plan. For her team, Ann decided to:

1. Clarify and commit to a strategy and objectives that would be the guidepost for deciding what to do or not do.

2. Delegate decisions and assign tasks to one person rather than multiple people to avoid duplicative efforts and communicate who is responsible for what to avoid confusion.

3. Focus part of her weekly team meetings on making joint decisions on what needs to be done, what can realistically be added, and what needs to be purged or put on hold.

Then, for herself, Ann committed to:

1. Time-bind her work so she could operate more from a place of "What can I get done in the time that I have?" rather than "I'm going to get as much done as possible for as long as I can keep going." This required her to let herself off the hook for what she didn't get done in a day.

2. Spend twenty minutes a day doing nothing, which would remind her of how she got to this place to begin with and, more importantly, build in a daily break.

3. Redefine what success meant, knowing this would be a long-term re-visioning that she would work on over time.

On its own, the belief that you need to get things done isn't a bad thing. We all need to do our work—always in a timely manner, and sometimes in a hurry—but it's when getting things done comes at the expense of our health, relationships, happiness, personal goals, or overall well-being that we get in trouble. To shift away from this hidden blocker, leaders need to focus on prioritization rather than productivity and let go of activities and to-dos that don't move the needle on what matters most. They also need to uphold healthy boundaries between work and personal time and engage in regular periods of downtime so they can fully detach from work and recharge their energy.

Coach Yourself

Ultimately, moving on from the "I need it done now" hidden blocker requires that, like Ann, we let go of a notion of success that solely anchors our self-worth and value in what we produce and how much we accomplish and, instead, adopt a more balanced view that supports our well-being inside and outside of work. Do you think this hidden blocker is currently holding you back? To start shifting your mindset, begin by identifying how this specific belief shows up for you and naming it. Then, reframe your belief in a way that supports a realistic notion of what you can accomplish in the amount of time you have.

From Blocked

- I need it done now.

- We need to finish this at all costs.

- I can't let up until everything is done.

- This has to be wrapped up as soon as possible.

- My value is determined by how much I accomplish.

- If I'm not busy, I'm falling behind.

- My success is determined by my productivity.

- There's always more I could be doing.

- Other people are doing more than I am.

To Unblocked

- My to-do list is not the measure of success.

- I will do my best to complete the work in the time that I have.

- My success is not solely defined by my productivity.

- I need to focus on what truly matters.

- My value goes beyond what I accomplish.

- Just because I'm busy doesn't always mean I'm productive.

To Action

- *Set realistic expectations.* Build limits around your work based on what can get done in the time you have.

- *Triage your tasks.* Prioritize tasks based on their impact, focusing on what truly matters rather than busy work. For the rest, delegate, delay, or let go accordingly.

- *Focus on outcomes.* Track how you spend your time to identify low-value tasks that can be reduced or eliminated.

- *Recharge.* Block off time to decompress and recharge.

Chapter 5

I Know I'm Right

If you are the smartest person in the room,
then you are in the wrong room.

—CONFUCIUS

Philip was the senior vice president of technology for a well-funded, growing startup that pioneered solutions in an untapped market. When Jill, the chief information officer, hired Philip to join the leadership team, it was because of his experience in taking technology ideas from inception to market, as well as the innovations he had led in his past roles. Jill called me after sharing her observations about Philip with her own executive coach, wondering if maybe Philip could benefit from coaching.

"Philip is great," she said. "This is not about fixing something that's broken. In fact, I can actually see him succeeding me one day. He's critical to our success, especially as we look to position ourselves for an IPO. But for us to meet the aggressive growth targets we've established, I need us to be moving like a peloton, in the original sense of the word. Because even one rider's behavior can significantly impact the outcome of a race."

In road-cycling races, a "peloton" refers to the main pack of riders that forms as they draft off each other to reduce wind resistance and improve overall efficiency. Teams use the peloton strategically to conserve energy and position themselves for key moments in the race, such as sprints or mountain climbs. Jill wanted her organization to work in the same way. "So where does Philip fit in this peloton?" I asked.

"That's the issue," Jill said. "A lot of times, he just doesn't. He always seems to be out front, on his own. It's always *his* way of doing things, *his* ideas taking center stage, *his* decisions being the final word. And what makes this so hard is that most of the time, he's right. He's incredibly knowledgeable, and his decisions get us where we want to go. But the way he communicates and the way he comes across is causing friction—with his peers and on his team, too. As good as Philip is, we simply cannot have this kind of dynamic from our leaders."

I asked her to elaborate on his communication style and describe how he comes across.

"He can be very condescending," Jill said, "and candid to the point of being rude. You know that expression about not suffering fools gladly? That's Philip. He has no tolerance for anybody he thinks is incompetent or uninformed, which is one of the reasons he always feels the need to weigh in. There was a meeting with senior leadership recently, where we apparently weren't moving fast enough for him. He went on a rant about how the solution was 'abundantly obvious' and why didn't we just do so-and-so and it would be resolved. He called out several people, including the person leading the meeting, for being ill-prepared, and said the whole thing was a waste of time!"

"Have you shared any of this feedback with him?"

"I have," said Jill, "but nothing's changed. I'm not sure he gets it. Or maybe he does, but he just seems to dismiss what I say. That would be a very Philip thing to do. So I'm hoping you can help. I really do think he's a huge asset to the company, and I want to see him stick around."

After our call, Jill had a conversation with Philip to reiterate her feedback, and to tell him she was invested in his success and wanted him to consider working with an executive coach to help him be a more effective team member.

That led to my introductory call with Philip, who acknowledged the issue Jill was seeing, but admitted he was only doing coaching because Jill had strongly recommended it.

"But there *are* a few things I could use some help on," he mused. "Like how to deal with mediocrity. I'd love to get your expertise on that."

This was a precursor of what was to come.

Philip Uncovers His Hidden Blocker

Philip went on to share that he had some roadblocks he could use some help getting past.

"What kind of roadblocks?" I asked.

"Basically, getting folks to move forward," he said. "Especially the rest of the leadership team. It's like we go around and around debating the same issues when it's clear what the path forward is, and yet we can't move toward it. It's really frustrating. Like right now, we're in budget season. And if each of the business divisions doesn't allocate part of their budget to support the sales technology upgrade we really need to keep up with our competitors, it's going to be a huge mistake. But instead of making a decision on technology spend and allocation, they want to discuss whether this is more of a training issue."

"Just so I can make sure I'm understanding . . . what's the roadblock here exactly?"

"*They* are! If they'd get out of my lane, we could just move on with it instead of talking about things they know nothing about. I hate to say it, but I question whether some of my peers have what it takes to be able to lead at this level and make the right calls. If you're an executive, you should be held to a higher standard. If you can't fulfill your role and be responsible with the position you've been given, then I don't think you should be there."

"OK," I said, "what I'm hearing you say is that *your* leadership challenges are happening because other people in your organization aren't capable enough."

"Listen, I would never say that to them . . . not in so many words, anyway. I'm direct, but I'm not cruel."

"I can appreciate that," I said. "But you're not disagreeing with what I heard from you?"

"Just between us, no. If everybody was up to snuff, I wouldn't be facing obstacles and delays every other day. *We* wouldn't be. Let me give you another example. We're in the midst of this huge push to increase head count. We had a leadership team retreat to discuss each division's personnel needs and how each leader was going to work with HR to get the right people in, but the conversation was all over the place with no clear agenda and definitely no next steps coming out of it. I mean seriously, how hard can this be? I tried to bring some direction to the discussion, but they just talked in circles. And sure enough, after the meeting, almost everyone there, myself included, had to have separate follow-up calls to clarify what to do next. Complete waste of time that could have been avoided if everyone had come prepared, instead of acting like they'd never done head-count planning before.

"Anyway, the issue came up at our executive team meeting a few days later—but as usual, only because I raised it. No one would address the elephant in the room, so I just came out and said our hiring meeting had been embarrassingly ineffective and inefficient."

"And how was that received?"

Philip laughed. "Not well at all! That was when Jill pulled me to the side to tell me I could have communicated with more tact to get buy-in. And probably why I'm here with you. I understand what she's saying, but I also think we can't fix problems unless we address them head-on. Feelings may get hurt, but we're not here to coddle each other. Our job is to solve problems and move forward."

"And so did your approach work?"

"It didn't. We're not an inch closer to a hiring plan, and actually we've probably moved a few steps back. And I'm even more frustrated."

"It's pretty interesting that the very thing you wanted, you actually ended up getting further away from."

"You mean regardless of what I did, we still ended up with no solution? I guess I can see that."

Now Philip got quiet.

"Hit a nerve?" I asked.

"Yeah," he said. "Because I know I'm right on what we need to do to solve our issues. And I'm at my wit's end trying to get through to them."

"You'll get there," I reassured Philip. "For now, I want to highlight the important insight you just made—that what you're doing is not getting you closer to your goal. Now we need to try to understand why that is so that you can course correct."

While Philip pointed out that his peers had difficulty moving to action, he couldn't quite see how *he* contributed to that dynamic. Many leaders like Philip, while extremely knowledgeable and often considered indispensable subject-matter experts, lack the self-awareness to realize that even the smartest person in the room has blind spots and the social awareness to realize they can come across as arrogant and dismissive. Alternatively, they may be aware that others find them condescending, impatient, or overly critical, but other people's opinions matter far less to them than being right does. Either way, these leaders can miss out on seeing multiple viable solutions that lie beyond their limited perspective, and they can struggle to gain buy-in from stakeholders who are told what to do rather than asked what they think.

Working with a leader who believes they are right more times than not isn't always easy. Their unwillingness to consider others' ideas or engage in fruitful deliberation shuts down the kind of dialogue necessary to gain buy-in, and it devalues others' contributions, sometimes to the point of precluding them entirely. Team members and colleagues end up not feeling heard, valued, included, or respected. This isn't good for work relationships, and it isn't good for engagement and productivity, either.

A study that analyzed data from more than 1.3 million employee reviews found that of all the negative workplace experiences employees cited, being disrespected had the most damaging effect on organizational culture. In these environments, workers were less engaged, less productive, and more stressed, and not surprisingly, more apt to leave.[1] What's the far better alternative? Time and again, studies show that the most effective leaders are those who treat people with respect, kindness, compassion, and humaneness, and who make a point to recognize others' contributions. The data demonstrates that leaders' positive attitudes and habits do much more than create a positive culture: their employees are more engaged, more loyal, more productive, and more motivated, which translates to a better bottom line and larger shareholder returns.[2]

By putting all his energy and focus into providing what he believed was the best answer—not to mention criticizing colleagues who took longer to find solutions or who preferred a more collaborative approach to decision-making—Philip lost sight of the damaging effects of his attitude and behavior. It's one of the most painful ironies of this limiting belief: even if this leader is right most of the time, the damage they cause to relationships and morale can be so harmful that it overshadows the immense value they bring and can even jeopardize their place at the organization. Just look at what Jill said about Philip: despite thinking he was critical to their success and so good that he had CIO potential, senior leadership was not willing to tolerate the dynamic he brought into the organization. It was too harmful to team relationships, to the growth of others, and even, ironically enough, to productivity, as Philip's insistence on his solutions created bottlenecks.

To help both Philip and me better understand how he was with his colleagues, I offered to shadow him at a few Zoom meetings, and suggested he record them so we could review his behavior later.[3] I gave both of us assignments. Mine was to jot down every time I observed Philip doing any of the following: listening, asking questions, interrupting, making an assertion, giving a directive, or providing context. I would also take note of his nonverbal traits, especially the tone of his voice and his facial expressions. Philip's assignment was to jot down how he was feeling and what he was thinking as the meeting unfolded—basically, his internal dialogue.

When we met next, we compared notes. I shared with Philip that based on my estimate, he'd spent roughly 70 percent of the time talking (rather than listening), he interrupted others on average nine times every half hour, and his most frequently used statements to respond to others were "I don't agree," "Got it," and "That doesn't make any sense." At first Philip, true to form, questioned my data, but when he watched some of the replays, he backed off.

"How about you, Philip?" I asked. "What did you write down about what you were thinking and feeling?"

"Well, most of the time," he said, "I was thinking we were wasting time, and I was feeling impatient. I was also feeling really frustrated and wondering why my colleagues can't just get to the point. I guess that's why I jumped in so often—we weren't getting anywhere! Like the marketing lead in that meeting—he goes on and on and clearly doesn't know what he's talking about. What am I supposed to do when somebody does that? Pray they'll eventually get around to a point? We could spend a lot less time in meetings if we'd just cut to the chase and get on with it."

"In that example," I said, "how much time do you think you saved by interrupting your marketing colleague?"

"Well . . . I'd say it saved us a few minutes."

"OK, let's say it's five full minutes. That's three hundred seconds. You and the team gained three hundred seconds. What do you think would have happened if you'd allowed your colleague to finish his thoughts?"

Signs You May Have This Hidden Blocker

What you may see and feel

You see what's coming before others do and don't understand why others can't see what's around the corner.

You have little tolerance for incompetence and get frustrated with others' lack of knowledge.

You get impatient with discussions to reach consensus and often find them circular.

You often feel confident about how to solve whatever problem is at hand.

What others may see and feel

You frequently debate points and insist on having the final word.

You don't listen well and have a habit of interrupting.

You are often two steps ahead and have little patience to bring others along.

Your tone can be clipped, condescending, or abrasive, and your body language conveys impatience (sighing, eye-rolling, tapping your fingers, shaking your foot or leg, fidgeting).

You take a "my way or the highway" approach and make decisions without exploring alternative solutions or without consulting others.

You're known as the subject-matter expert or the person with the deepest institutional knowledge but not as a leader.

"I mean . . . it's possible he could've eventually arrived at the same answer I did, or maybe the follow-up discussion would've netted out in the same place. Or, we could have landed nowhere."

"Always a possibility," I said.

"I guess we'll never know," said Philip, "because I didn't let it play out. I'll tell you, I rarely do, because I almost always know what we need to do, so it doesn't make sense to wait and cross my fingers that someone else will come up with it. I mean if *I know I'm right*, why wait?"

"So, is that what drives you? Being right?"

"Yeah, I think so. I probably sound a bit too confident, but in many instances, I know I'm right, and if my colleagues honestly examined my track record, no one could disagree. I haven't been proven wrong very often."

"I think everyone recognizes that you know a great deal, Philip. The question is how your belief that you're right is helping you get any closer to your goals, because from everything you've told me, it doesn't seem like it is."

"Well, at this moment," Philip said, "I'm not sure. How about that?"

We both laughed.

Philip Unpacks His Hidden Blocker

While Philip got to the belief that was holding him back, he wasn't ready to accept the collateral damage it was causing. So I took a slightly different angle with him.

"Here's what I'd like you to do," I said. "You know how you watched the meeting replays? I want you to do that again, but this time, watch from the perspective of everyone else. Pick two or three folks and jot down what you think they're feeling and thinking as the discussions unfold, particularly as it relates to you. And also what you see them doing verbally and nonverbally."

"I can already tell you what I'm going to see," Philip retorted.

"How come I'm not surprised you said that?" I laughed. "Why don't you keep me in suspense and tell me next time, *after* you go through the exercise."

A few days later, I got this email from Philip:

> *Hi Muriel–*
>
> *I reviewed the videos using your assignment. Probably not surprising to you but watching from others' perspectives was eye-opening. I didn't realize how much I shut discussions down. Looks like I suck all the air out of the room! We need to work on this because now I get what Jill has been saying, and it's obviously not good. I'll share more when we meet but wanted to give you a heads-up.*

Philip elaborated at our next session.

"OK, that was not easy to watch," he began. "The looks on everyone's faces said it all."

"Which was what?" I asked.

"That they were pissed! Or at least very frustrated. With *me*."

"And why is that?"

Philip sighed. "Because I am clearly a serial interrupter. I didn't realize how often I was cutting people off and hurrying them along."

I nodded. "I saw that too. But let's stick with your observations for a little longer. Tell me more about the looks on people's faces and their body language."

"Well, I saw some sighing, and some glancing at each other, after I spoke. And some people looked deflated. But the worst was at one point, Jill actually covered her face with her hands, like she couldn't take it anymore. That's not what you want to see from your boss.

"But the other thing I saw is that I am literally coming off like the kid in the classroom jumping out of his seat to get called on by the teacher for every question," he said. "Actually, it's even worse, because I don't even wait to get called on and just blurt out the answer every time. Or I rush to correct the other students if they get it wrong. And everyone else is annoyed and doesn't say anything, because why bother. I watched the videos and was like, 'Oh my god, I'm *that* kid.' I told my wife about this, and she kind of looked at me and was like, 'Um, this is news to you?'"

"And what do you think the impact is?"

"Well, clearly it makes others not want to speak up. So then I jump in even more. Then we're in this vicious cycle. And it doesn't help any of us get closer to a solution because the more I push, the more they distance themselves. It's like I'm on one side of a very long table and everyone else is way on the other side. My sense is they probably see me as an adversary instead of someone who's trying to help all of us achieve a common goal."

"And is that how you want to be seen?"

"No, it isn't. I want what's best for the company and for us to get to our objectives, but my colleagues probably think I'm just looking out for what's best for me and the tech group. And look, I don't need to win any popularity contests, but I do want to be respected and trusted to do the right thing. And not just because that's how I want to be known as a leader but also because, heck, it would probably make my job a lot easier if these folks didn't feel like I'm just out to get them."

"How so?" I asked.

"There'd be less tension and maybe they'd be more open to my suggestions and willing to discuss them directly versus having back-channel conversations. At the end of the day, I need these folks to buy in, and I can see how my pushing doesn't exactly do that."

"What gets in the way of you using more of a buy-in approach?" I asked.

"I just get so frustrated!" said Philip. "Executives should know what to do, right? Why are they in this position if they can't make the calls they need to?"

"You expect them to have answers. They don't. It frustrates you. So you interject. Do I have that right?"

"Pretty much."

"Makes sense," I said. "Look, at the root of most frustrations is an unmet expectation. But when we watched you in those meetings, it didn't seem like your colleagues had a chance to give much, if any, of their perspective because you tend to swoop in before anyone else has a chance to."

"I'm just trying to save us time and preempt the inevitable going around in circles that lead us to nowhere. Is that such a bad thing? Isn't driving to solutions what leading is all about?"

"Tell me more. What makes you think that?"

Philip shared how some of the best leadership training he'd ever had came from being a natural disaster emergency responder, something he still did on a volunteer basis. "Out there in the wild," he said, "you *have* to know what to do. You can't wait to make the call, because these are life-or-death situations and there's no room for error."

"Do you believe the same holds in your leadership role at work? Is it life or death in those meetings?"

"I see what you're getting at. I'm approaching these meetings with a similar level of urgency and intensity. And expecting others to do the same."

"And as a result of that?"

"To me, the discussions feel like a waste of time because every minute that goes by, the greater the risk. I want everyone to come to the table with answers. And I expect them to trust me with my solutions. I'm in emergency response mode even when we're not in a life-or-death situation—which in fact we never are."

"Now we're getting somewhere, Philip. You're seeing how your rules of engagement as a leader in one scenario don't apply in another. Do you see how it's shaped your core assumption about how leaders should operate?"

"I've definitely believed leaders should have all the answers," he said. "To me, that shows leadership. Or at least that's what I've always thought and how I've always led."

Philip paused to think.

Potential Costs of This Hidden Blocker

Impaired decision-making: Leaders who insist on their point of view may miss out on seeing a range of viable answers or an innovative solution. And by limiting or preventing others' participation, they miss out on hearing others' ideas. Without considering the full context or others' input, they risk making decisions prematurely.

Alienated stakeholders: An unwillingness to hear others' ideas and opinions makes peers and team members feel devalued, disrespected, and excluded. Rather than feeling brought along, they feel pushed along.

Damage to team morale: Team members who aren't listened to or included in decision-making and problem-solving suffer from disengagement, low motivation, and lack of buy-in.

A culture of learned helplessness: If a leader establishes a pattern of swooping in and providing the answers, team members become overly reliant on them and don't grow and develop.

Stunted self-development: Leaders who are convinced they know everything also don't grow and improve, because they don't think they need to.

"I've gotta say, though, if that's not what leadership is, then I don't know what is."

"So basically who are you as a leader if you're not constantly churning out solutions? How do you add value?" I asked.

Philip sighed deeply. "Exactly."

The Roots of This Hidden Blocker

If you take a look at most school systems, it's no wonder that many of us believe that we primarily bring value by being right. Students don't get top grades and achievement awards for exploring possible solutions to a problem or alternative ways of approaching a question, but for producing the correct answer. Sometimes, students are even penalized for asking too many questions or for not responding right away, because they are thinking before they speak. And to be admitted to postbaccalaureate institutions in most parts of the world, a rite of passage is to sit and take exams for hours or sometimes days to demonstrate all you know. Much of what our educational system teaches us is that our worth depends on how much we know—how many answers we get *right*.

Now, this is no knock against expertise and excellence, which all great leaders need. But being a subject-matter expert does not necessarily make you a leader.

My first job out of college was in a coveted management development program. While I was there to learn how to be a manager, it was very clear to me that the way to gain favor was not only to figure things out on my own but to be proficient in offering solutions, whether in my lane or not. I recall an incident where a colleague was reviewing the latest market analysis at a team meeting and he was misinterpreting the data. Rather than help him figure out the error, I flat out told him he was wrong, corrected him, and then proceeded to roll my eyes when I realized he still didn't understand the data. He felt embarrassed, and it created tension that impacted my work with him. And, yep, that incident made it into my performance review.

As so often happens, the drive to push for the right answer starts early, and my case was no different. My family reinforced the notion that being smart was highly valued. My dad, a man born into humble beginnings in a rural village in Haiti, was sent away to school at a very young age. He shares the story of living with another family, away from his own, so that he could get an education. He would wake up very early every day to study before heading off to school a few hours later. My dad excelled in school, through college and graduate school, and went on to have a lauded international career. But it's clear to me that while he became a subject-matter expert in his field, he pinned much of his identity on his knowledge—and never left much room for others to possibly be as knowledgeable as him.

You can only imagine how that played out, at work and at home. There was never much asking . . . just telling. Family dinners were about who was right and who knew the most. None of this was intentional; it never is. It was merely a continuation of what my dad learned to do at a young age. So I too learned that in order to make myself valuable, I'd better always be able to prove myself right.

That belief, like many, dies hard. Particularly so because this one is strongly reinforced by the people around you. Parents and other caregivers, then teachers and professors, give you accolades for the knowledge you can display, and being smart can earn you awards and recognition. At work, proficiency can propel you up the ranks, and bosses and managers or anyone else who will benefit by leveraging your knowledge love to have you around. Not to mention that the more you can be autonomous, self-sufficient, and come up with answers, the more valued you are. Why? Because it frees up others' time and provides them with an in-house expert. Your expertise makes their lives easier. The approval you receive becomes reinforcing, and you continue being everyone's problem-solver.

Like Philip, when we have the belief of "I know I'm right," it's often due to a strong identification of our self-worth with being known as "the fixer." When others value us for solving their problems, it's easy to get attached to that validation, and then to build our identity around being the smartest person in the room. The more situations we face where being right yields a positive outcome, the more we default to believing, as Philip did, that that's our main value contribution. While the source of this belief can be different from one person to the next, here are some typical experiences that can lead to and reinforce this hidden blocker:

- You were rewarded and recognized for coming up with solutions independently and faster than your peers.

- You were praised a lot for having the right answer, whether at school, on teams, or even among your friends.

- You were often told that you were smart and publicly recognized for it.

- You excelled academically and as an individual contributor.

- You rarely failed and had few opportunities to learn from failure.

This last point brings up a special challenge for those with the "I know I'm right" hidden blocker: the times they're actually *not* right. No one likes to be wrong, especially publicly, but for people with this hidden blocker, it can feel catastrophic. It's not just a matter of encountering a gap in knowledge that can be easily remedied—to them it's a serious negative judgment on their abilities and self-worth, and they feel it acutely.

Regardless of the experiences that led you to develop this particular belief, chances are that as a result, you operate with "single-loop learning," a term coined by the late Chris Argyris in his now classic article "Teaching Smart People How to Learn." Argyris, widely regarded as the father of organizational learning, says that most people equate learning with problem-solving and assume that "the well-educated, high-powered, high-commitment professionals [in] key leadership positions" are the best at it. But not so fast. While solving problems is important, he goes on, it's too narrow a definition of learning, as it means we never move beyond the stage of finding and fixing issues in our external environment. A more expansive form of learning, one that enables continued improvement over the long term, is what Argyris calls double-loop learning, which focuses not just on external problem-solving but includes self-reflection. The self-reflective learner is able to realize if and how they're actually contributing to any of the problems in their environment and can thus change their behavior to prevent those problems, rather than just react to them and do damage control.

Philip was a classic single-loop learner. He was an excellent problem-solver, and he brought a lot of value to his teams and organizations for his ability to laser in on solutions. But he was also focused on the externals and on one, and only one, answer—his. That meant he was missing out on the self-reflection that could increase his awareness and enhance his leadership, and he reacted with defensiveness if his answers were ever challenged. It never occurred to him that he could possibly be contributing to some of the problems at work, or if there were better solutions than the one he was wed to.

When we're operating with the "I know I'm right" hidden blocker, it becomes difficult to distinguish between having *the* answer and having *one of* multiple viable solutions—and it causes us to miss the enormous value of being able to ask the right questions. "In a complex world," leadership experts Steven D'Souza and Diana Renner remind us, "no one person can possibly have all the answers. You will inevitably face challenges that are hard to define, let alone solve—even after years of management experience."[4]

Double-loop learning can help us move beyond the strictures of this hidden blocker by redefining our role as leaders: from problem-solvers focused exclusively on the externals to introspective thinkers who ask the questions that lead to the best possible solution in a field of options. To me this is the most exciting part of moving from single-loop to double-loop learning and breaking free of this belief: we are now open to the possibility for solutions from any source, including out-of-the-box ideas that can lead to breakthrough achievements.

Philip Unblocks from His Hidden Blocker

Philip was now questioning whether there were other ways he could contribute as a leader. I asked him if we were to observe him in a leadership team meeting in the future, what differences he would like to see.

"I'd want to be less adversarial," he said. "Basically I'd like to be on the same side of the table as my peers rather than the opposite side."

"OK, that's a great visual," I said. "What would need to happen to make that come to life?"

"More open dialogue where people feel comfortable contributing," he said. "I'd speak less and listen more, and I'd be more patient and receptive to what others have to say. If I put myself in their shoes, I can see how coming out of the gate with a critical tone would shut them down. I do want to invite more discussion, but I also still want to make sure we arrive at the best solution, and that's never going to change."

"What could your role look like in these meetings so you can do *both*?" I asked.

"I think it would be for me to influence people rather than pressure them to comply," Philip said. "I'd be functioning as more of a guide, leading others to the best collective solution, rather than offering it to them."

"That's helpful, Philip," I said. "So instead of leading with 'I know I'm right,' what belief can help you move to their side of the table, where you still lead, but you lead collaboratively and speak in a way that invites their contributions?"

"How about 'I guide others to find the best solutions'? I like the idea of being a guide—the person who shines a light so others can find their way but doesn't do the finding for them. If I go in with that attitude, it will help me keep my expectations in check and give me a better way to approach conversations and interactions."

"I love it," I said. "It makes you open to the best solution from whatever the source."

"I hear you," he said. "There's a possibility that someone else could come up with a better solution. I need to give it a chance."

Not every leader who holds the "I know I'm right" belief starts out as a command-and-control leader who preempts discussion and jumps in to solve problems. It can happen slowly over time, as the leader's knowledge base increases and institutional knowledge becomes more siloed, and as others become more dependent upon them. It's positive reinforcement with a negative consequence: the leader who provides all the right answers is rewarded with expanded authority and ownership, while those they work with succumb to learned helplessness, reduced engagement, and lack of autonomy. The leader's time is then eaten up with providing answers and solutions, which undermines their own mandate and frustrates their opportunity to scale. Short on time and patience, they adopt a "my way or the highway" approach and lean on giving directives, rather than offering up suggestions the recipient can follow up on or options they can choose from.

As we saw with Philip, an effective reframing for the "I know I'm right" hidden blocker is anything that de-emphasizes the leader as sole authority (that is, guide versus commander, solution supporter rather than problem-solver) and encourages collaboration (that is, facilitator rather than answer provider, delegator rather than individual contributor). When a leader takes this approach, they ask more questions and are willing to take a broader perspective. They become more approachable, because they're willing to say, "I'm not sure, but what do you think?" or simply, "I'd love to hear your take on that." It encourages others to contribute, which leads to better engagement.

To put his new belief into practice, ahead of his meetings Philip made a practice of visualizing himself as a guide on the same side of the table as others, whether they were his direct reports, the leadership team, or outside stakeholders. He used that image going forward, which helped him adopt the tone, attitude, body language, and words to use to remain on the same side of the table even when he could feel the urge to assert his perspective.

Philip's visualization practice was a powerful mental tool to keep his attitude oriented in the right direction, and to keep his new belief aligned with his desired impact. And of course, as beliefs always influence behavior, it was instrumental in helping him actually show up as a leader who guides and collaborates. Now it was time to identify specific actions he could take to remain unblocked.

For Philip, a lot of this came down to discerning when to provide the answer, when to guide others to find the answer, and when to leave it entirely up to them. There will always be times when a

TABLE 5-1

How should I respond?

When to give answers and/or directives	When to ask and listen
Use in situations with high urgency and/or high risk	Use in situations where reframing or shaping the discussion to get to a solution is needed while still keeping others engaged
Goal: Achieve maximum efficiency and mitigate significant risk	Goal: To influence and collaborate to achieve a cocreated solution
When to hold back	**When to guide**
Use in situations where others are sufficiently skilled and empowered to come up with an answer and/or it's in the scope of their role, not yours	Use in situations where getting buy-in and alignment is important, and/or building others' future capacity is important
Goal: Granting autonomy to others; freeing up your time to apply to areas where you will provide more value as a subject-matter expert or leader	Goal: To have others feel engaged; to expand others' skills and knowledge and have the capability to come up with the answer

solution is needed right away, and in those moments, making the call without hesitation is a valuable asset. But because Philip's default mode was to immediately give the answer in all situations, and because that behavior had been reinforced for years, the process of knowing when to step in, and to what degree, took some practice.

We ended up creating a tool to help Philip choose his level of responsiveness based on the urgency and risk of the matter at hand, as well as on the specific goal to be achieved. Many of my clients have found this tool helpful (see table 5-1).

Philip continued to have slip-ups in his communication style from time to time, which was certainly to be expected. But he remained committed to his new belief and his new set of actions. Toward the end of our coaching engagement, I could see more flexibility in him—he argued his point less and interrupted less often—but I knew he was really making progress when I heard two things.

The first was from Jill. "Philip is so much easier to work with," she said. "There's a confident humility there that, honestly, I didn't think he was capable of. He sits back and listens and lets other people talk first. I can tell he doesn't always like it. But he does it because he sees the value. I think he's learned that he doesn't have to weigh in on *every single thing.* He's letting others offer solutions, and if he has a better idea, which he often does, he says it at the end, after everyone has had a chance to speak. Even if we end up going with Philip's idea, it comes off more like everybody got there together, rather than him issuing edicts from on high."

The second was from Philip himself. "The leadership team is way more capable than I was giving them credit for," he said. "And get this—I purposely took a back seat for a new initiative we have going on. When an issue came up at our last meeting, I made suggestions but did not push my answer as the only solution—which I think surprised everyone. And it was great to see some of my colleagues pick up the ball."

Having subject-matter expertise and the ability to laser in on a solution is a great skill for any leader, and a valuable asset for teams and organizations. But much depends on the manner in which leaders convey that knowledge. For leaders like Philip, the belief that they are always right prevents them from being able to lead from the same side of the table as their peers. The most effective leaders believe that the best answer lies in the sum of the parts and therefore are able to offer their knowledge in a way that builds trust and consensus and that encourages others to offer their own ideas and solutions. Learning to function as a guide rather than a problem-solver, and a facilitator of dialogue rather than solely as a problem-solver, is key to their continued success.

Coach Yourself

If you find yourself identifying with any part of Philip's story, you may be getting blocked by the belief that you have all the answers, or that you are the only one with the *right* answers. If "I know I'm right" seems to be the hidden blocker that's currently holding you back, begin by identifying how this belief shows up for you and naming it. Then, reframe your belief in a way that feels authentic to you and supports actions that will explicitly encourage and value others' contributions and help you unblock from this limiting belief.

From Blocked

- I know I'm right.

- I have all the right answers.

- I know more than anyone else here.

- I'm always right.

- I know exactly what I'm talking about here.

- I wouldn't say it if I wasn't sure.

- They should trust me given my track record.

- I'm absolutely certain about this.

- I'm never wrong about these things.

To Unblocked

- My role is to help others find solutions, not always give them the answer.

- Asking the right questions is just as important as offering the right answer.

- I gain commitment by asking for solutions rather than compliance by telling them what to do.

- My solution is not always the only solution.

- I'm confident in my ideas, yet I'm open to other perspectives.

To Action

- *Make room for others.* Refrain from always being the first to speak.

- *Engage in active listening without interrupting.* Focus fully on what others are saying to understand their point of view before responding. Use WAIT (Why Am I Talking?) before speaking to determine if your participation is necessary.

- *Share your reasoning and invite feedback.* Provide context, explain how you arrived at your conclusion, and welcome input to help identify areas for further consideration.

- *Ask open-ended questions.* Use questions like "What do you think?" or "How do you see it?" to invite others' input.

Chapter 6

I Can't Make a Mistake

You have to confront the brutal facts of the reality
that you might not pull it off.

But at the same time have unwavering faith.

And you have to do both at the same time.

—JON BATISTE

"The past year has been utterly exhausting," Kristin said. "Between dealing with the fallout from The Great Debacle and having to keep the division going *and* taking over for Ben, it's been a lot."

"The Great Debacle" was how Kristin and a few of her close colleagues referred to the tumultuous past year at their company—an unfortunate situation involving toxic leadership and unethical behavior. The discovery that the company's finances had been mismanaged led to a huge shakeup, resulting in the abrupt resignation of the CEO, as well as the ouster of the CFO and several other members of the executive team—including Kristin's boss Ben, the senior vice president of the commercial division. Though she had always been next in line for the role, Kristin had not expected to move up this soon, and certainly not under these circumstances. Now she was leading a group that, like much of the rest of the company, was still reeling from the damage done to its brand and culture, and understandably distrustful of leadership. Quite a few people had resigned, but Kristin felt a deep responsibility to stay and take part in the efforts to rebuild. By the time I met Kristin, she had been with the company for a total of seven years, and in her SVP role for one.

"I can only imagine how difficult this has all been," I said. "Now that you're a year in, how are you feeling about your new role?"

"Believe it or not, I think I'm exactly where I should be," Kristin said. "I've always loved this company, and I actually feel honored to help bring back a sense of normalcy. There are a lot of really good people here, and they're still angry about what happened. I am too, and it makes me all the more motivated to right the ship. I'm extremely committed to restoring our reputation and making things better for everyone."

"It sounds like this is very purpose-driven for you . . . and that you've assigned yourself a heck of a big job," I said. "I hear you on wanting to make things better, though. How is that going so far?"

"Well, I do know that morale is better—certainly much better than a year ago. But as far as how *I'm* doing, I'm not sure, and this is one of the things I was hoping you could help me with. Leadership is still coming out of damage-control mode, and my boss is so overwhelmed, we barely have time to catch up. My team's performance is solid, but as far as how they find my leadership, I'm not sure of that either. I check in with them regularly and I've asked for feedback, but mostly what I get is questions about what the future holds. I'm worried that means I haven't done a good job of allaying their uncertainty, which has made them hesitant to share what they really think with me."

"I can understand you wanting to know what they think of you," I said, "especially after all that's happened and how much staff has lost trust in leadership. Why don't I talk to some of the folks you work with and see if I can get some actual feedback for you?"

"That would be great," Kristin said. "I've been going at this without a playbook, so I'm really interested in hearing what I can do better."

Kristin struck me as conscientious, loyal, and honest. I admired her empathy and her willingness to support others through the collective upheaval they'd experienced. It was clear she had deep affection for the employees and would work tirelessly to advocate for them, whether they were in her division or not. Her attitude toward herself, however, was a different story. The more we spoke, the more it seemed she was dismissive of her own contributions and inclined to be hyper-self-critical. I suspected she was way more forgiving of others' missteps, but not so tolerant of her own. I was curious if that was indeed the case.

Kristin Uncovers Her Hidden Blocker

I spent the next few weeks talking to Kristin's employees, her peers on the leadership team, and after several rescheduled meetings, her boss. I did find many of them reluctant to offer critical feedback, but not for the reason Kristin wondered about. Their hesitation came from genuine appreciation for and loyalty to Kristin. Employee after employee praised Kristin's open and generous communication style and her willingness to listen and provide support. Even her boss wanted to emphasize Kristin's strengths rather than areas she could improve, repeatedly telling me the division couldn't have made it through the last year without her. Once I assured everyone that Kristin had specifically requested this feedback as a way of supporting her development as a leader, they were more forthcoming.

When I sat down with Kristin to share what I'd heard, she was bracing herself.

"So how bad is it?" she asked.

"Oh, wow, Kristin," I said. "What's with the doom and gloom? You know what? I think I'll have to keep you in suspense. Let's start with what folks say they appreciate about you. Because guess what? They really *do* appreciate you."

"Well, that's nice to hear," she said. "They're all very kind."

"They are, but I think it's more than that," I said. "One of them made a comment that was really striking, and to me it sums up people's feelings toward you: they said you gave this organization 'the warm hug it needed after the torment it had been through.' I don't know that I've ever heard a comment like that."

A look of embarrassment swept across Kristin's face. "That's great," she said, "and thanks for passing that on, but what about the less touchy-feely stuff? Like my real leadership impact."

"I'll give you that part too. But I want you to realize that what that person said directly reflects your leadership impact."

"OK," Kristin said, "I hear you."

I took Kristin through the two major themes that highlighted the strengths her team had identified in her, and what they most valued in her leadership. I handed her a feedback report with a distillation of their remarks, supported by some of the comments they made:

1. Collaborative and empathetic leadership approach

- "She is very committed and available. Her door is always open, literally and figuratively."

- "She's deeply human and relatable and cares about what you're talking about."

- "The level she made herself available to staff during the crisis is above and beyond. . . . It was actually a brilliant decision to put herself out there as a model for trustworthy, ethical leadership."

- "She listens very closely and shows tremendous empathy—she single-handedly shepherded our organization through a crisis. Everybody is in awe of how she was able to take a full-body blow with such grace and poise."

- "You can tell she's actively listening and absorbing every word you say. When she reports back or asks a follow-up question, it's amazing to see all that she's able to take in."

2. Strong intelligence and strategic thinking ability

- "She's unbelievably intelligent and has a huge capacity for information."

- "She's smart, grasps issues quickly, and can connect all the dots."

- "She's a quick study. She is fantastic at synthesizing views and distilling what she hears from others."

- "She is smart, with a good sense of strategic ability to think through complicated issues."

- "When Kristin leads a meeting or assigns new projects, you can tell she knows the agenda or the objectives backward and forward. Her preparation skills are unmatched and whatever she produces is flawless."

This is the kind of feedback leaders live for. But not Kristin. She looked more and more uncomfortable, and I could tell it was a struggle for her to receive it. I asked her how she felt about the feedback.

"It's all really great and I appreciate everyone's kindness," she said. "But I'm waiting for the other shoe to drop. I'm eager to hear what they said I'm doing wrong and how I can improve."

"We'll get there. But the feedback you asked for includes your team's estimation of what's working well. I hope you won't just dismiss it. What's clear is that to others, it's a big deal that you listened and brought a collaborative approach to leading the group. Does that resonate with you?"

"Well, when I took over the role, the place was a mess," she said. "Not just my division but the whole company. Nothing like that had ever happened here before, and I've never seen people so upset. I just didn't think going about business as usual was the right thing to do. So I spent my first thirty days having one-on-ones with each person in my group."

"Every single one of them?"

"Yup. All ninety-three of them. And then I expanded to the rest of the company. I think I've met with at least half of the folks in head-quarters individually, and I traveled out to the regions for town halls to hear our other offices' concerns. Sometimes I was definitely the punching bag, but I can take it, and I think it's important to hear from everyone to rebuild that trust."

"I'm sure it *has* helped rebuild trust," I said. "Let's finish the feed-back report and look at the suggestions people had for you. What was interesting with your feedback, Kristin, is that typically I get at least three or four opportunity areas for leaders. For you, I only got one. Can you guess what it is?"

"No, just tell me—I don't even want to try because I'll probably get it wrong."

"It's not a test, so there's no penalty if you get it wrong. But what kept coming up time and time again was everyone wants you to work on your decisiveness."

Kristin's jaw dropped. "What? My decisiveness?"

"Yes, and that was the case across the board—your team, your peers, and your boss, too. Now listen, this isn't about the quality of your decisions; it's more about how long it takes you to get to them. Or even if you make a decision at all. Here, let me show you what they said, and you can see if any of this rings true to you."

Just as before, we went through the list together:

- "Kristin needs to work on making decisions. She does a tremendous amount of research on her own, followed by a lot of canvassing to find out what others think, which creates delays. We've been late to deliver a few times, so people are starting to get frustrated and move ahead on their own. The irony is Kristin is so smart and everyone trusts her judgment, so she shouldn't hesitate to make the call."

- "I would love for her to take a tougher stance and just put a stake in the ground. Sometimes it feels like she's kicking the can instead of driving to a conclusion."

- "It's so nice that she wants to hear from everybody, but there are certain times she needs to make the call herself. I also think she has a perfectionist streak that can get the best of her and makes her put off decisions."

- "Her strong desire for consensus often supersedes her decision-making. It can really slow things down."

- "She often gets bogged down by others' input. She has to be able to seek input from the right people versus trying to hear from everybody before she'll commit. She relies too much on others for assurance that she's making the right decision."

- "I've noticed she's often in search of the perfect decision or answer. That's admirable to a certain extent, but 'perfect' doesn't exist, and her drive to get there just ends up causing delays."

- "She's very risk-averse because she doesn't want to make any mistakes. Sometimes she's slow to act because she's working so hard to make sure everything is exactly right, or because she's asking everyone if they think she's making the right call."

"Wow. That's not good," Kristin said. "I had no idea so many people think I'm so bad at making decisions."

"I don't think that's what the feedback says," I told her. "It says they'd like you to drive to decisions faster than you are. It's not saying you're making bad or *wrong* decisions. It's about pace."

"Same difference in my view!" Kristin said. "This is one of my primary responsibilities, and I'm failing at it. But how am I supposed to make the right decisions if I don't take the time to listen to what everyone thinks? I mean they just said they like that I listen to them, but then they turn around and say, 'Oh, don't waste your time listening to us and just make a decision already.'"

"Is that your only takeaway, Kristin?"

"No, I'm sorry. I'm just surprised and frustrated. It hasn't been easy spending all this time meeting with people, getting input and hearing their complaints, and then to be told I'm not doing it fast enough."

"I understand. And I don't want you to lose sight of the fact that all that listening you did *was* needed. Now they need you to take all the information they've given you and do something with it."

"OK, I can see that," she said. "I guess I've been so busy trying to gain consensus I haven't really done the one thing they're looking for me to do—make the decision." She sighed. "It's not like I don't *want* to make decisions. I just think it's important to get input and to weigh different perspectives."

"To what end?"

"To make the *right* decision. That's the end goal."

"And how will you know if you're making the right decision?"

"Well, that's the thing. I'm not sure I know what the right decision is in many of these situations. And I sure don't want to make the wrong one, so I keep deliberating and asking for input until I feel sure we've come up with the right answer that everyone is onboard with, together. There've been enough bad calls made for this team. Hell, for this company! And I'm not letting that happen again—not on my watch. I can't make a mistake."

"Hmm. You can't make a mistake, so you spend more time looking for the right answer *and* for confirmation that you have the right answer . . . and then end up never making the decision that could potentially cause the mistake to begin with?"

Kristin laughed. "Well, when we play it out like that, I suppose that's what's happening. This all boils down to the fact that *I can't make a mistake.*"

"Is that actually a *fact*, though, Kristin? That you can't make mistakes?"

"I guess it's not a fact. Everyone makes mistakes, obviously. I just *feel* like I can't."

Signs You May Have This Hidden Blocker

What you may see and feel

You focus on what needs to be fixed or improved and negate or downplay everything that's good.

You're hard on yourself when things don't go the way you think they should.

You have an all-or-nothing approach: you only want to engage in something if you feel you are going to do it well. If not, why bother?

You're seldom satisfied with the end result, even if you've devoted significant time and effort to it—and even if others think the results are good.

You often compare yourself to others and feel like you're not as successful or effective as them.

You tend not to share your perspective unless it's fully formulated.

What others may see and feel

You sometimes slow down progress because you don't take a stance or put a stake in the ground.

You second-guess your decisions and are too easily influenced by what others think or by their pushback.

You leave no stone unturned and spend an excessive amount of time trying to dot every *i* and cross every *t*.

You frequently brush off compliments or respond by pointing out your own shortfalls.

You fail to delegate, preferring to do everything yourself to make sure it's perfect.

Kristin Unpacks Her Hidden Blocker

Because leadership and high achievement work hand in hand, the hidden blocker of "I can't make a mistake" tends to be on heavy rotation among my clients. Sometimes it shows up as the strong aversion to and fear of making mistakes, as was the case with Kristin. This type of thinking is powered by the desire to avoid failure, so naturally it inspires avoidance behaviors—for example, Kristin's reluctance to make decisions and her procrastination on moving things along. Other times, this limiting belief shows up as an active pursuit for impossibly high standards. Instead of avoidance-driven thinking like "I must not make an error" or "If I don't try, I won't risk getting it wrong," the thinking behind those who put enormous effort into trying to achieve perfection is more along the lines of "Nothing less than perfection will do" or "If I don't meet all my goals, it means I've failed—and I can't let that happen."

Perfectionism, which some of Kristin's team had mentioned, can be very challenging to work with and overcome. Certainly, it exists on a continuum, and at the lower end of the spectrum—what we might call perfectionist tendencies—it doesn't necessarily result in behaviors that compromise one's leadership or well-being. To underscore the point, some experts distinguish between *adaptive* and *maladaptive* perfectionism. With adaptive perfectionism, a person sets very high goals and standards that are challenging but not unrealistic. If they fail to meet those standards, they're disappointed, but they're able to tolerate their mistakes or shortcomings, then regroup and try again.

Maladaptive perfectionists, on the other hand, set unrealistic goals, and they feel intense distress when they miss the mark. Even small errors can feel disastrous and can inspire harsh self-recrimination and shame. Maladaptive perfectionists may have such an intense fear of failure that they procrastinate on tasks or avoid trying at all, and when they do produce good results, they're unable to derive satisfaction from them. Other researchers, including renowned perfectionism experts Paul Hewitt and Gordon Flett, argue against the notion that perfectionism can ever be considered adaptive or beneficial, as it is never without its problems. They caution that we should not conflate the desire to excel with the desire to be perfect. These are two very different things, and because it is impossible to reach perfection, anyone striving for it is engaged in an unachievable quest that sets them up for exhaustion, chronic stress, and greater vulnerability to psychological distress.[1]

I appreciate this point, and to be clear, the drive to excel, avoid mistakes, and succeed is healthy and desirable—indeed, it is characteristic of good leadership. The problem comes when these healthy desires become a preoccupying force that inspires unproductive behaviors (procrastination, inaction, harsh self-criticism, overwork, indecision), or when a person sets unachievable metrics for success.

Experts tell us that how perfectionism affects our behavior depends on the patterns of thinking behind it:

- *Self-oriented perfectionists* are internally motivated. They set impossibly high standards for themselves that they strive constantly to achieve. They can be extremely self-critical and focus excessively on their own shortcomings.

- *Socially prescribed perfectionists* are externally motivated. They believe they must achieve impossible ideals in order to be valued and accepted. They have a deep fear of disappointing others.

- *Other-oriented perfectionists* set impossibly high standards and expectations for others. They constantly evaluate others' behavior and performance, and can be very critical when others miss the mark. (We'll be taking a closer look at other-oriented perfectionism in the next chapter.)

Do you see the common theme with each type? Perfectionists strive with all their might to make the impossible happen. Even when they realize they're in a losing game with ever-shifting goalposts, perfectionists cannot resist trying. "Maybe this time I'll finally feel like I've succeeded." "If I hit it out of the park, maybe this time they'll see how valuable I am." "Maybe this time they'll deliver the performance I know they're capable of." Their core fear is of not measuring up to themselves, to others, or both.

The thin line between a healthy personal desire to excel and the type of limiting belief that makes success and satisfaction feel out of reach appears when leaders set impossible standards for themselves, and doing so negatively impacts their effectiveness or well-being. That's what was happening with Kristin. Though she was undoubtedly successful and well-liked, and had many strengths, her need to avoid mistakes was compromising her effectiveness in her new role. And in the saddest of ironies, it was beginning to eat away at the trust her employees felt for her.

Until this point, Kristin had justified her belief that she can't make mistakes as necessary given the turmoil they had just been through as a result of previous leaders' decisions. What was still unclear was whether this hidden blocker of hers was isolated to this particular context and moment in time, or whether it also showed up in other ways. So I gave Kristin a simple assignment.

"I want you to try something between now and our next meeting," I said. "I'm going to send you a jar and some marbles. Starting next Monday, I want you to put a marble in the jar every time you notice the thought 'I can't make a mistake' cross your mind. At the end of the day, text me a picture of the jar. Do that every day of the week."

I knew this would be logistically possible given that Kristin was on a hybrid schedule, and she'd be working from home.

As the week progressed, Kristin sent me pictures (see figure 6-1).

When we next met, I showed her a printout of the photos side by side. "OK, Kristin," I said. "What's going on here?"

We both laughed.

FIGURE 6-1

Kristin's jar exercise

| Monday | Tuesday | Wednesday | Thursday | Friday |

"As hokey as I thought this jar thing was going to be," she said, "it was really enlightening."

"In what way?"

"Well, first of all, check out the empty jar on Monday. I didn't forget my homework, and it's not that the thought of 'I can't make a mistake' never crossed my mind, but every time I went to put a marble in the jar, I hesitated. I kept wondering if I'd understood the assignment correctly. I almost texted you to ask. Anyway, I kept going back and forth in my head, with my hand literally holding a marble over the jar, and then gave up. Is that ridiculous or what?"

"Not at all," I said. "What did this tell you? How did it translate into real life?"

"It made me notice how, even with small, inconsequential things, I overthink it because I don't want to do it 'wrong,'" she said, gesturing air quotes. "To the point where I don't make a move. And then let's not talk about what happened on Wednesday." She rolled her eyes.

"Which was?"

"Well, notice how on Tuesday I finally put some marbles in the jar. But then, by Wednesday, there were fewer than the day before."

"What's that about?"

"I took some marbles out!"

Now that one, I had not expected.

Kristin shook her head. "Once again, I started to worry I was doing the exercise wrong. Then I started second-guessing whether or not I'd really had the 'I can't make a mistake' thought, and I took out a few marbles."

"Interesting."

"That's not interesting, Muriel. It's called flip-flopping, being wishy-washy. Over marbles! No wonder my team is frustrated with me. I hate to admit it, but I think I do this a lot. With every decision—big, small, medium, whatever."

"But then by Thursday, you're back."

"Yeah, seeing the patterns visually made me realize what was happening. So as soon as I saw that, I just committed. And as you can see, 'I can't make a mistake' is at the top of my playlist when it comes to my personal soundtrack."

"Bravo for seeing it through, Kristin, and even more importantly, for drawing some very powerful insights from the exercise. What I hear you saying is that this belief you have that you can't make a mistake occurs frequently, even on inconsequential things, and it gets in the way of you moving forward or causes you to doubt yourself when you do take action."

"That's right," Kristin said. "And I can see how this has happened over the last several months in terms of me not committing on some key decisions I need to make for our group. But even more than that, I think this fear of making a mistake makes me spend way more energy than I need to on a lot of things, which slows me down. I'm kind of embarrassed by it, to be honest."

"Why's that?"

"I don't like being wrong," she said. "Who does? And in this exercise, I'm damned if I do, damned if I don't. Whether I put marbles in or not, I look bad."

"Look bad to whom?"

"To you?" Kristin replied. "And me too!"

"Can you say more?"

"I don't want to look like I don't know what I'm doing. I mean who does? So I go out of my way to make sure my work is foolproof."

"Is that what would happen if you made a mistake? It would mean you don't know what you're doing?"

"Well, in my *mind*, yeah."

Kristin explained that she'd been raised with a "do it right or don't do it at all" mentality. In a lot of ways, that had helped her enormously. Her performance reviews were consistently outstanding, she'd received merit increases every year, and she'd been promoted three times in seven years. "None of that came about by accident," she concluded.

"You ought to be proud of yourself," I said. "I'm curious—did you ever receive *any* negative feedback?"

"A few things here and there on performance reviews," Kristin said. "Everybody has areas for improvement."

"And how did that affect you?"

Kristin laughed. "Not well! I mean, in feedback discussions I was always super professional, and I was genuinely grateful to know how I could get better. But yeah, for any metric where I didn't get a five out of five, it was all I could think about."

"How did it make you feel?"

"Disappointed. It's like I came up short and I just wasn't good enough."

"So, is it the perfect score that you're chasing? Or is it the feeling of being good enough that it gives you?"

Kristin stayed silent.

"There's no right or wrong answer here," I assured her.

"Yeah, I know. I'm just realizing how much all that I do is not for the work in and of itself. It's to keep me from feeling lesser than. And if I can't be assured that won't be the case, then I just procrastinate or avoid the task entirely."

"Lesser than what?"

"Lesser than what I think others expect of me. And what I expect of myself. Except that now I realize that in my desire to not disappoint

Potential Costs of This Hidden Blocker

Indecision, inefficiency, and inaction: Research has found that perfectionism is linked to forms of self-sabotage such as procrastination and poor time management. Fear of making a mistake can lead to obsession over details, delays in starting a dreaded task, and missed deadlines as the leader labors to avoid mistakes.[a] Leaders may avoid a task altogether if they think they can't execute it flawlessly.

Intolerance of risk: Leaders who fear making mistakes may play it too safe and resist trying anything new or unfamiliar, which stifles creativity. Fear of not being the best may keep them from trying at all.

Lack of focus and full engagement: While leaders in pursuit of perfection can become overly focused on their assignments, they often have trouble focusing in meetings and conversations because they're so preoccupied with perfecting their response or worrying that they'll make a mistake. With their mind elsewhere, they're unable to listen fully, take everything in, and respond productively.

Diminishing returns: Despite their high attention to detail and ability to work long hours, research suggests that those with

others, I've avoided making decisions. Which means that in reality, I *have* disappointed them because I haven't made the decisions they need me to make."

The Roots of This Hidden Blocker

A close friend of mine, Anthony, recalls how when he was very young, he loved hanging out with his dad as his dad worked on his car. While Anthony wanted to spend time with his father, have fun, high levels of perfectionism seldom outperform their nonperfectionist colleagues. Why? Researchers speculate that perfectionism is a form of "counterproductive overstriving."[b] As one commentator put it, perfectionists "over-improve to the point of negative returns."[c]

Poorer mental and physical health: Multiple studies have found that perfectionism is linked to anxiety, depression, insomnia, low self-esteem, burnout, and even eating disorders and premature death. The causes are complex, but one clear link is the high stress associated with perfectionism, which takes a toll on mental and physical wellness.[d]

a. Laura Dorwart, "Understanding the Psychology Behind Perfectionism," Verywell Health, September 19, 2023, https://www.verywellhealth.com/perfectionism-5323816.

b. Simon Sherry et al., "Perfectionism Dimensions and Research Productivity in Psychology Professors: Implications for Understanding the (Mal)-Adaptiveness of Perfectionism," *Canadian Journal of Behavioural Science* 42, no. 4 (2010): 273–83, https://doi.org/10.1037/a0020466.

c. Robinuel Olewole, "Unpacking Perfectionism: Understanding Its Causes and Effects," CoachHub, July 25, 2023, https://www.coachhub.com/blog/unpacking-perfectionism/.

d. Olewole, "Unpacking Perfectionism."

and maybe pick up a thing or two about auto mechanics, his dad's goal was to fix the car as quickly as possible so he could get on with his day. Needless to say, their different agendas didn't mesh well. If Anthony asked too many questions, his dad would tell him to quiet down and focus—something that's hard for most young children to do. If his dad asked him to hand over a tool and he grabbed the wrong one, his dad responded with a few choice words of disapproval. But what really stuck with Anthony were the times his dad allowed him to help with a small task and he didn't do it right on the first try. "You don't know what you're doing!" his dad would say. "Go on and play somewhere else."

Was Anthony's dad a horrible person? No. He was a very busy adult who was frustrated to have to spend his one day off working on his car. And like most of us, he was probably doing the best he knew how.

But his "get it right the first time or don't bother" attitude wasn't confined to weekend car repair—it was his general approach to life. Inevitably, it left an indelible impact on Anthony, who to this day takes an all-or-nothing approach to every task. Either do it well or don't do it at all—much like Kristin and many other successful people who struggle with the need to get everything exactly right. In Anthony's case, striving for perfection served him well academically and professionally, and his clients now benefit from his meticulousness.

But where it doesn't serve him is in efficiency, because he applies the same level of "getting it right at all costs" in all areas of his life. Anthony is well-liked, but he often frustrates his colleagues because the level of precision he devotes to every step of the process is non-negotiable. There's always something he feels he could've done better, and he often feels dissatisfied as a result. He's had similar issues at home, as no home renovation project is ever complete because Anthony can't stop tinkering.

The origin of the "I can't make a mistake" hidden blocker often stems from how much permission you were given to make mistakes in the past—at home, at school, with your friends, at work. If you were rejected or made to feel ashamed when you made a mistake or didn't measure up, the desire to avoid reexperiencing that feeling will be extremely strong, often irresistible. It can push you to avoid error and the accompanying pang of disappointment or shame by procrastinating, or simply not trying. Think of the time you didn't apply for a job or ask for a promotion because you didn't want to face the possibility of not getting it, which would confirm in your mind that you were a failure. Alternatively, it can push you to chase achievement, always aiming for better, faster, higher in a never-ending quest to eclipse your last accomplishment and prove to yourself or others that you are valuable and deserving of approval. Perfectionism, says research psychologist Brené Brown, is not about healthy striving or the pursuit of excellence. It is an unhealthy, unproductive way of thinking and feeling that says, "If I look perfect, do it perfect, work perfect and live perfect, I can avoid or minimize shame, blame and judgment."[2]

Another root of this hidden blocker is driven by comparison. Theodore Roosevelt told no lie when he said, "Comparison is the thief of joy," and yet comparison is everywhere around us. In our hypercompetitive culture, we measure our worth in how we stack up against others. In class rankings. In talent reviews and performance evaluations. In how quickly we rise through the ranks or how much money we make. On the leaderboard on your Peloton bike. In the number of followers and likes we amass on social media.

The message we absorb is that we're only as good as the person right beneath us and never as good as the people ahead of us. Constantly comparing yourself to others as a source of validation can make you feel like mistakes aren't an option and that you must always outperform others to be valued, and there is plenty of evidence that this form of socially prescribed perfectionism is on the rise, especially in younger generations.

Psychologist Thomas Curran, a recovering perfectionist himself, says that perfectionism is driven by "deficit thinking": we feel that we're flawed, defective, or imperfect in some way, and so we try to repair that deficiency through achievement. When Curran was featured on the TED *WorkLife* podcast, host and bestselling author Adam Grant related his own story of perfectionism. Back in college when he was a competitive diver, Grant's team presented him with the "If Only" award. "If only I had pointed my left pinky toe," Grant explained, "I would've gotten an eight and a half instead of an eight. . . . I would not leave the pool because I always felt like there was something I could have improved." And while we may admire Grant's diligence and laugh along with him at his team's tongue-in-cheek award, his quest for perfection was, in his own words, "maddening." Curran explains why: "The way that [we] perfectionists are built," he says, "makes us very sensitive and vulnerable to those set-backs and failures, which occur all the time, because it's a threat to that idealized version of who we want to be and who we think we should be." The gap between reality and that lofty ideal, which re-mains elusive, can create a lot of anxiety and self-criticism, and can prevent perfectionists from pushing themselves out of a comfort zone in which they know they can excel. The ironic consequence, con-cludes Curran, is "they don't necessarily succeed in the long run."[3]

Failure, unhappiness, or dissatisfaction due to perfectionism are not foregone conclusions, however. Countless leaders who have strug-gled with perfectionism have learned how to achieve success without sacrificing their health and well-being. Curran and Grant are two well-known examples, both having become renowned leaders in their fields. And while most of us, including Anthony and Kristin, likely won't become household names, every perfectionist can do the work necessary to examine the unique source of their "I can't make a mistake" hidden blocker, which will reveal their own path to break free from it.

Kristin Unblocks from Her Hidden Blocker

With Kristin's increased awareness of how her focus on not making mistakes was limiting her, she was ready to move on. But to *what* was the question. I asked Kristin how she'd like to operate in the future.

"I want to be able to consistently drive issues to closure," she said. "I still want to hear and be thoughtful about others' input, but I want to be the decision maker I'm expected to be at this level. I want to make decisions more quickly, and with more confidence. I can't use data gathering or consensus building as an excuse for not mov-ing things forward, when in reality it's my fear of not getting it right that's stalling us."

"Let me ask you a question," I said. "How will you know when you've found the perfect answer?"

"I really don't know. I have no idea what that feels like because I've never found it! It's always ahead of me."

"And why do you think that is?"

"Because perfection isn't actually attainable?"

"Exactly. But excellence is."

"I see what you're saying," Kristin said. "I've been treating this like an all-or-nothing—it has to be perfect or it's a total failure. And I've also been acting like making zero mistakes will get me to that never-achievable state of perfection."

"Let's shift the conversation from perfection, which we agree isn't attainable, to what is—excellence. What do you need to pursue excellence instead of perfection?"

"Having a set of standards to aim for," Kristin said. "That would make it more concrete and achievable. When I reach them, it will be a concrete signal that I can move forward, instead of overthinking everything and worrying that I've made a mistake."

"I like that," I said. "The fine line you're drawing is that you're going to start playing to win rather than playing not to lose. Do you see the difference?"

Kristin gave me a genuine smile. "Yes, I really do. Playing to win is about pursuing excellence and holding myself up to high but *attainable* standards. Standards that increase the chances we get to the best answer, not a perfect answer. But playing not to lose is totally based on my fears. I try to guarantee perfection by avoiding mistakes at all costs. Which in and of itself is a losing battle because it keeps me backed up on the ropes instead of in the ring."

"But now you know that," I said. "And that's huge. Before, you were leading without awareness of this limiting belief, and it was impeding your progress and your team's, too. Now that you know the 'I can't make a mistake' belief keeps you in avoidance mode, what would help you make decisions collaboratively without getting caught up in analysis paralysis?"

"I might revise this later, but I think it's something like, 'I will do the best I can with the information and resources available to me.'

That allows me to still be discerning while being realistic about what's possible. And it also makes me focus on what's in my control—because sometimes mistakes happen that have nothing to do with me or that aren't in anyone's control."

As Kristin's tendency was to ruminate over decisions and get stuck in the process of gathering data and gaining consensus, I suggested that she create a decision checklist. This checklist ensured that she was moving forward by having her rely on an established decision process rather than on her tendency to move the goalpost as she got closer to having to put a stake in the ground.

When Kristin came to our next meeting, she took an index card out of her planner.

"Here's what I pulled together for the checklist," she said. "It puts natural parameters in place to keep me in check instead of swirling and chasing perfection."

1. *Frame the issue.* Define the problem I'm looking to solve or the question I'm trying to answer.

2. *Determine criteria.* List the conditions that need to be met to bring the issue to closure in a way that is "good enough."

3. *Engage others.* Involve only those who are directly affected by the decision or need to approve of the final outcome.

"These are the three areas that tend to keep me stuck because I get worried I've missed something," she said. "So I figured if I'm able to put a deadline against each one and focus on completing them and crossing them off my list, it will move me forward."

What was important for Kristin, and anyone else who tries to avoid making mistakes at all costs, was to have a clear path to an acceptable resolution, with deadlines to keep her honest. Having interim milestones also helps get out of the "all or nothing" trap by recognizing the progress you're making toward a goal, rather than focusing on the goal itself. And by setting realistic expectations,

Kristin released herself from doing everything she could to avoid failure to doing the best she could with the information and resources she had.

Then Kristin surprised me by turning her index card over. Written in large capital letters was "NOT ALL MISTAKES ARE CREATED EQUAL."

"I realized that for me to stop fearing mistakes so much, I need to become more comfortable with actually making them," Kristin said. "And the best way to get used to something new is to start small. Obviously, I'm not going to let up on mistakes that would have a huge impact, but if I make a small mistake—a spelling error, let's say—I will survive."

"Ah, taking baby steps in getting more comfortable with what makes you uncomfortable," I said.

"Exactly," said Kristin. "And this little index card is a big reminder for me—there are different types of mistakes, and I shouldn't be treating them all the same. A spelling error is hardly the same as botching a $50 million decision."

Kristin had alighted on something critical as she assessed how to circumvent her mistake avoidance. And that was the idea of aligning her energy and efforts with the risk associated with different types of possible mistakes. The lower the risk, the less energy to give the task or decision. The higher the risk, the more attention to pay to it. To use her examples, she really didn't have to spend so much time and energy repeatedly combing through reports and memos for issues. She could reserve that time and energy for the areas of greater consequence—the high-stakes decisions.

It also helped to work through "What's the worst that could happen?" scenarios. Kristin and I did this together at first, because of her tendency to overestimate the consequences of even low-stakes mistakes (that is, missing a meeting would not result in her team losing faith in her; not being able to answer a question was not an indication of "incompetency"). Working through worst-case scenarios with a trusted partner is always an illuminating exercise and, believe it or not, can even be comical. (Let me tell you, once you can laugh at the words of your inner catastrophizer, you are all but released from the tall tales it's spinning.) Here's what this exercise can look like:

Muriel: Pick a mistake you recently made.

Kristin: I forgot to include certain people during my thank-you remarks at the latest town hall.

Muriel: What's the worst that could happen as a result of that?

Kristin: They get really upset and don't want me as their leader anymore.

Muriel: And if that happens? Then what?

Kristin: I'll have to quit and then I won't get hired anywhere else. And I'll end up destitute!

Muriel: Really? All that from not saying thank you?

Kristin: I know, I know! "What a tangled web we weave," right?

Muriel: Right! So, let's revisit. What's the worst that could *really* happen if you forgot to thank those folks?

Kristin: They could get upset and think I was careless.

Muriel: And what could you do so the end of the story doesn't end up with you being jobless and destitute?

Kristin: [laughing] I could follow up with an email to acknowledge my mistake and thank them publicly. That way, they still get the acknowledgment, even if it's belated.

Muriel: Can you live with that?

Kristin: Well, I wouldn't like it because I'd still be disappointed in myself, but sure I could live with it.

Muriel: How do you know?

Kristin: Because the feeling will pass, for one thing, and no matter what, I know I can work through it—even if I don't like it.

This exercise works with any type of catastrophizing, that well-known "thought trap" that has you believing the absolute worst will happen: one mistake means you're totally incompetent, a coworker's failure to greet you one morning means they hate you, your boss asking for a meeting means you're about to get fired. Once you bring your thinking out into the open through a dialogue with a trusted partner (writing your thoughts can help, too), you can usually see how distorted and unproductive it is. And yes, sometimes you can even appreciate the humor in your thinking.

This is how Kristin discovered that the worst she could suffer from small mistakes was a fleeting pang of disappointment. And that the worst-case scenarios she was envisioning for bigger mistakes with more serious consequences actually weren't realistic. She also realized that while all mistakes had consequences, none were an indictment about her true worth as a person.

Learning to become more realistic about the risk involved with potential mistakes went a long way in allaying Kristin's deep fear of making mistakes, which was holding her back. But when Kristin realized that this fear also played a significant role outside of work and had made her feel stuck for a long time in a lot of areas of her personal life, part of her necessary work also involved therapy. There, she explored and processed the family and intergenerational origins of her fear of failure as well as the trauma that the most recent organizational shakeup had caused her, more deeply than we could through coaching. Our work centered on her professional context, and Kristin continued to use her decision checklist to help her gain greater confidence in making decisions.

"I'm really trusting my own judgment more," she told me one day, "and I can see it's making a difference in the team's output, too. We haven't been late on a deliverable a single time this entire quarter."

Kristin also became very mindful of when "I can't make a mistake" and the ensuing doubts came creeping back, until she finally landed on a reframe that supported her to drive to action no matter what the uncertainty: "Let me do the best I can with what I have. And if I don't get it right, I have full confidence I'll be able to figure it out."

Coach Yourself

Kristin learned that failing in and of itself was not the catastrophe she believed it to be—and that was a good thing, because we're all going to fall short from time to time. It's how we respond to our failures, large and small, that makes the difference. We don't use these occasions as reasons to beat ourselves up, give up, or despair. Instead, we learn to give ourselves grace and to use our mistakes for the inimitable occasions for learning and improving they provide. We learn, as Harvard professor of management and leadership Amy Edmondson puts it, to fail intelligently. "It is natural to want to avoid failure," she says. "But when we avoid failure, we also avoid discovery and accomplishment. The only way to succeed in any endeavor worth trying is to be willing to experiment, to try new things, knowing full well that many of them will yield failures. We have to embrace those kinds of failures because that's where great advances and even joy come from."[4]

Do you recognize some variation of the "I can't make a mistake" hidden blocker in yourself, from equating small mistakes with failure to a dread of making an error to full-blown perfectionism that keeps you obsessively checking and rechecking your work?

Begin by naming the way this belief shows up for you, then identifying a reframed belief that helps you let go of perfectionism and self-recrimination. Finally, embrace actions that will help reinforce your new belief and put things in a more realistic—and more self-compassionate—perspective.

From Blocked

- I can't make a mistake.

- I have to get everything right.

- Anything less than perfection is unacceptable.

- I can't allow anything to slip through the cracks.

- I have to be certain before moving forward.

- There's no room for error in what I do.

- Mistakes are unacceptable in this environment.

- If I make a mistake, it could ruin everything.

- Getting it wrong isn't an option for me.

- I can't afford to mess up.

To Unblocked

- My focus is excellence, not avoiding failure.

- Mistakes are not failures.

- Imperfect action can be better than no action.

- Not all mistakes are equal.

- I don't have to be perfect to be successful.

- Even if I make a mistake, I can handle the outcome.

- Perfection isn't required for good results.

- I can still contribute and add value, even if I don't get it right every time.

To Action

- *Set realistic expectations for yourself.* Create a decision-and-completion process that outlines clear steps to keep you moving and requires you to check off items as you make progress. Set achievable goals rather than aiming for perfection.

- *Put things in perspective.* What's the worst that can happen—realistically—if you make a mistake? Most of the time, it's not nearly as bad as we fear.

- *Prioritize progress, not just results.* Recognize and reward the effort, even if the outcome wasn't perfect.

- *Practice risk-taking in small ways.* Deliberately try things outside your comfort zone to build confidence in handling mistakes and learning from them.

- *Focus on solutions rather than regrets.* If you make a mistake, shift quickly from analyzing the error to brainstorming constructive steps forward.

- *Practice self-compassion when mistakes happen.* Treat yourself with grace as you would a friend, reminding yourself that everyone makes mistakes and that mistakes don't define your abilities.

Chapter 7

If I Can Do It, So Can You

We do not see things as they are, we see things as we are.

—ANAÏS NIN

Robin is the chief development officer of a large nonprofit she'd joined several years ago. She was now being strongly considered to succeed the CEO and founder, who had alerted the board that she would transition out of the CEO role in the next couple of years. As part of the succession-planning process, the board and CEO had commissioned executive assessments of the internal candidates, which would be followed with coaching to support them in developing any focus areas that emerged from the feedback. The goal was to give each candidate the opportunity to prepare for the CEO job and put their best foot forward for the role itself. Robin had elected to work with me as her executive coach throughout this time.

Ahead of my kickoff meeting with Robin, I met with Diane, the CEO, and Tony, the chief human resources officer, to ensure we were aligned on the coaching process, especially in light of the tie-in to succession planning. I also wanted to get their initial perspective of Robin and where she stood relative to being Diane's potential successor.

"Robin is fantastic," Diane began. "I could really see her taking this organization to the next level. She's super strategic and a natural visionary, and we need that as the organization moves into its second quarter century. She's also got really strong financial acumen—she gets what it means for us to have a sustainable financial model, and she can raise money like no other. That's a rare combination. Which is actually one of the things that's top of mind when it comes to choosing a successor; I've been the face of this place for so many years, the one donors associate us with. So, when I step away, it could leave us with potential financial vulnerability.

"On top of all that, the media loves her. Donors love her. She's an amazing communicator, and that's really helpful in being able to tell our story and show people why our mission is so critical right now and into the future. So I really want this process to be one where she knows we believe in her and want to invest in her, because she brings so much. If we didn't believe in her as a strong contender for CEO, we wouldn't be doing this."

"Is there anything about Robin becoming CEO that concerns you?" I asked Diane.

"This is not meant to take away from everything I just said, but I think Robin might be a little rough around the edges at times with her team and peers. I haven't seen it myself, but I've heard about it. And she can't afford to be like that. I know she does a lot, but she's got to be a little easier on folks when she's stressed."

Tony elaborated after Diane left for another meeting. "It's more than a little rough and it's not just around the edges," he said. "I don't know if Diane is downplaying it because she really hasn't seen much of how Robin treats her staff, or if she just doesn't *want* to see it. Either way, Robin can be tough as nails. I've had folks come into my office in tears. But the strange thing is, people still really like her. Because she can also be very charming, loyal, and supportive."

"I can see that," I said. "When I first met her, I definitely sensed that she has that charismatic aura that can draw others in. She's good at telling her story and seems very passionate about the work and cares about the mission. I see how that can be endearing. So what causes the tears?"

"It's just when she's off, she's *really* off, and it stings. She expects a lot from people, and when she doesn't get what she's looking for, she can be harsh and impatient. Plus, with Robin, you're never quite sure what you're going to get because she can be hot and cold. Now mind you, she's always great with Diane or the board, and definitely with our donors. But with her peers and her team? Different story.

"I agree that Robin brings some really strong attributes as a potential CEO," Tony went on, "but the fact of the matter is, whoever takes that seat will personify the culture of the organization. And I don't think Robin's tone is what we want or need to set. Plus, I worry many folks would see her being promoted as an endorsement of that type of behavior. I could see us losing strong talent over it, which obviously is not what we want, especially at such a critical point."

"Has Robin been given any of this feedback? How aware is she of how she comes off and the noise it's creating?"

"We went through an exercise a few years ago where the entire senior leadership team did 360-degree surveys," Tony said. "Afterward, every leader met with their teams to share their learnings and commitments moving forward. Everyone except Robin. She's typically an out-front type, but for this she definitely stayed pretty quiet. So maybe that 360 gave her some of this feedback? I don't know. What I do know is that Diane and I have had conversations with her about the importance of being able to motivate others, and she says all the right things, but nothing really changes in terms of how she behaves. Because she gets results. We've raised more money every year since she's come on board than we have in the history of this organization. But I can tell Diane is worried because she doesn't want the culture she's built for the past few decades to be trampled overnight by her successor."

"It sounds like Robin's success in one area is excusing her shortcomings in another."

"One hundred percent. I admit I've been guilty of giving her a pass too, but this kind of behavior will not get her to CEO."

Robin Uncovers Her Hidden Blocker

At my kickoff meeting with Robin, it was clear to me that either she lacked self-awareness of the issues that Diane and Tony had mentioned or she simply didn't want to acknowledge them, because she never brought them up. When I asked what she wanted to get out of the executive assessment, her focus was on how to drive the organization toward future growth.

"I want to understand what the appetite is for radical change for this organization," she said. "We have so much potential to broaden our impact, but I'm not sure everyone sees it or wants to do what it will take to get there. I'm also interested in gauging whether there's overall buy-in to the fundraising model we've built over the past couple years."

"Got it. But I just want to make sure you understand that this assessment is about *you*," I said. "It's an opportunity to get further insights on you as a leader and potential successor to Diane, not on how everyone else is doing or how they can level up."

"Oh, yeah, of course," she said, with a reassuring smile. "I definitely want to know where I stand. I have a lot to offer, and I'm committed to this place, but you know, if I'm not the right person, I'm not the right person. So that would be good to know too."

"Well, the assessment won't be evaluative in terms of saying whether or not you're the right person. But it will give you some data so you can better understand what it will take to be the CEO here, and where you stand relative to those expectations. And if there are any gaps, you can decide if you want to work to close them as preparation to potentially lead this organization one day. Make sense?"

"Yep. Let's do it."

With that understanding, I launched the assessment, which for this purpose was a rather lengthy process of interviewing a wide range of stakeholders that Robin, Diane, and Tony had selected. I met with board members, donors, peers, direct reports, and even some skip-level individuals further down in the organization.

The feedback was revealing, to say the least. Stakeholders uniformly agreed that Robin was extraordinary when it came to fundraising and being the public face of the organization, but her behavior inside the organization was a different story. In essence, she was perceived as harsh, impatient, and frequently unsupportive with employees. Based on this feedback, it was clear that Robin was going to experience serious challenges in earning the trust she'd need to inspire followership—and to set a tone that would uphold the kind of culture that left employees feeling inspired and appreciated, rather than dismissed and inadequate.

Here's some of what I heard from her peers and staff:

- "She has to work on how she manages and interacts with direct reports. She can't have a tone that's biting, sarcastic, or angry. It undermines trust and makes her intimidating. She's also unpredictable—you're never sure if you're going to get praised or scolded. She needs to have more patience and consistency now, and definitely if she were to be CEO."

- "Her style can be off-putting, especially to junior staff. She doesn't realize the impact of her words and actions on people. It would help if she would ask questions and listen like she means it and actually try to find the value in others' contributions. She can be so dismissive."

- "When there's an issue, she shouldn't call out people in public. It doesn't support the culture of collaboration we have here. She should have the tough conversations, but not in a way that embarrasses people."

- "When Robin gives feedback, you can come away feeling like you got hit by a bus! Despite what she seems to think, we're all working hard, and she doesn't realize how motivating it would be to hear what we're doing well. She can't just let us know when something goes wrong or highlight someone's shortcomings. Focusing on the negative all the time is very discouraging, and honestly, it ends up making *her* look bad as a leader."

- "I'd be very concerned if she became CEO. I wouldn't want her attitude and style filtering down from the top and infecting the whole culture. She can be very intimidating and condescending."

- "It would go a long way if she acknowledged that the team works hard and gets great results. Robin loves to focus on the negative, and she makes us feel like if we're not here all the time, we're not fully committed or maybe even lazy. I wish she'd understand that we're all plugged in and can trust us to get the job done."

Unfortunately, this was not the first time I'd heard feedback like this about a leader, but it was worrisome in its own right, especially because Robin seemed to be blithely unaware of how she was perceived by the people she needed to inspire and motivate, and of how she made them feel. One person told me point-blank that if Robin became CEO, she would resign.

Not surprisingly, walking Robin through the feedback report made for a very tense meeting. She sat quietly throughout it, but her body language—crossed arms, clenched jaw—radiated irritation. When we got to the end of the report, she turned the document face down on the table.

Though the answer was pretty evident, I began with my usual question. "How is all this landing with you?" I asked.

"Not great, obviously!"

"I know this must be tough to hear," I said. "Can you tell me more?"

"What do you want me to say?" she said, her voice rising. "This is total BS! That's what I can tell you."

Robin went on to say that if it weren't for her "ridiculously high" expectations and "constant vigilance" in holding the team accountable, they would never have had record-breaking fundraising campaigns, year after year. "A lot of it in a down economy, I might add!" she said. "How do you think we were able to avoid layoffs? How do you think we were able to pay bonuses? No one was complaining about any of that, were they? And our service to the community didn't lapse *once*—in fact, we were able to serve *more* people during the pandemic, thanks to the increase in funding. Do people think I just conjured that money up out of thin air? We had to work for every penny! Nobody cares that I'm overworked and exhausted, do they? Do they think this is easy, having to be on everyone all the time and constantly checking in and then having to go pound the pavement every day in search of funding? Unbelievable."

Robin let loose with a few choice words as she continued to grapple with this unwelcome feedback. Thankfully for both of our sakes, it was late on a Friday afternoon. Once she was done, I suggested she take the weekend to reread the report and process the feedback.

"I also want you to give serious consideration to the question of whether you *really* want to be CEO of this organization," I went on. "And Robin, over the weekend, there's just one rule: no discussing the feedback with anyone between now and the next time we meet." I didn't want to run the risk of Robin taking her frustration out on anyone. "Do you think you're up for the task? And do you think you can hang in there until Monday, when we can get some more clarity?"

"Yes," Robin said. "I can do that. And, for what it's worth, I appreciate you pulling all this data together. I'm not sure what to do with it just yet, but I guess you'll be helping me with that too."

When we met on Monday, Robin was much calmer.

"So, where are you now?" I asked.

"First of all, I'm glad you specifically told me not to talk to anyone, because it took all of my resolve not to. But that question you asked me, 'Do I really want to be CEO?' stuck with me all weekend. Because until now, the answer was 100 percent yes, with total confidence. I never even considered anything but an automatic yes. It just made sense, you know?"

"And now?"

"Well, on Friday I was ready to say to hell with it. Why stay at a place where I'm not even liked?"

"Is that what you—"

"I know," she interrupted. "I know there's much more to it than that. But as for the question of wanting to be CEO, I've actually come back to a yes, though I'm not nearly as confident about it as I was before. I love the work and I love the mission, but this feedback makes me wonder if I have what it takes. When it comes to people, I mean. Diane has shared with me that there was a time when she had to work on her people skills and leadership style—that she was more of a strategy, big-picture person and it didn't come naturally to her to inspire and motivate people. But it became a necessity as the organization grew, in terms of head count as well as our reputation. We're operating on a national stage now, and Diane is the public face of this organization. Anyway, I guess that was her way of telling me I needed to work on my people skills too if I wanted to be CEO one day. But I had no idea it was this much of an issue."

"What exactly is the issue that you see?"

"My approach might be getting us great financial results, but that alone won't get me to CEO. There's a big disconnect there. If I truly want to be CEO, I've got to address how I'm making people feel."

Robin admitted that motivating and inspiring others was important, and that she was grateful for everyone's efforts. But beyond compensating people fairly and occasionally thanking someone for their extra effort, she conceded that she rarely expressed gratitude. "I'm not one to go around thanking everyone or handing out trophies

Signs You May Have This Hidden Blocker

What you may see and feel

You have very high standards and expect others to meet them and are frustrated when they don't.

You feel responsible for pointing out what you see as others' shortcomings.

You are often dissatisfied with others' results and get irritated when they deliver something different from what you expected.

You hold others to a high standard because you just want the best for them and motivate them to be the best they can be.

What others may see and feel

Others find it difficult when you review their work because you nitpick, give too much feedback, or are overly critical.

You often criticize others publicly.

Even when you're trying to help, you tend to show your frustration to get others to perform.

You tend to blame others when something goes wrong.

You are inflexible and rigid in how others should go about their work.

You are frequently disappointed with others' performance and don't hesitate to let them know.

You say you want one thing but are not happy with what you get.

just because they did what they're supposed to do," she said. "I think we're just supposed to do the work, you know?"

"I think a lot of this is about being acknowledged more than anything," I said. "Your staff needs to know that you see what they're contributing and that their work is making a difference."

"OK," she said. "That makes sense, and I can work on that. The other part, though, about motivating and inspiring, and all those things they said about my tone and attitude, will be a lot harder. I get frustrated a lot because I don't think people are doing what they're capable of. And it shows because I don't have a poker face. I'll give you an example. Our communications director had to pull together a simple press release about a strategic partnership we're launching with a major brand. I asked to see a draft before it went out, and the thing was a disaster. It didn't name all the components of the partnership, and it didn't list everyone who was involved. I also didn't find some of the wording particularly compelling. I mean come on, he's the comms *director*. If I can pull together a halfway decent press release, why can't he?"

"And is that what frustrated you?"

"Well sure! I believe in someone until I don't. And most times, I give people the benefit of the doubt. Look, I don't ask anyone to do anything I wouldn't ask of myself. My principle is *if I can do it, so can you*. It's not that complicated."

Robin Unpacks Her Hidden Blocker

When clients are having trouble seeing (or accepting) what's blocking them, it's helpful to drill down into the impacts of their behavior. It struck me that the best way to do this was to let Robin herself tell me.

"So, Robin, let me make sure I understand," I said. "You assign a task. You think it's a reasonable ask because, hey, if you can do it, they can too. Then they don't deliver. What happens next?"

"Well, when they don't follow through, I guess I sort of lose my cool a little bit."

"And that looks like . . . ?"

Robin frowned. "It looks like what happens when anybody loses their cool. I get frustrated. And I let people know it."

"How?"

"Maybe just a bit of a direct tone. But mostly, what I do is let them know how they've fallen short or not stepped up, and I correct them, which is part of my job. But it's probably my least favorite part of the job. It constantly frustrates me when folks deliver substandard performance."

"What standard do you have in mind, exactly? Do you want them to meet the standard needed to get the job done, or meet the standard of what *you* can do? Because that's not always one and the same."

"What are you trying to say, Muriel? Not everyone's like me?" Robin joked.

"Hard to believe, Robin, but sadly, the answer is no," I responded, laughing.

"Point taken," she said. "But is it wrong for me to have high standards for my staff? I would think that would be motivating, wouldn't you? I mean if you expect mediocrity, that's what you tend to get."

"What is the difference, if any, between holding others to high standards and holding others to your capabilities?"

"I'd say high standards are based on some objective, observable measure of accomplishment. And holding others to my capabilities . . ." Robin paused as she thought about it. "I guess that's based on the expectations I have of myself. But I don't get why that's a bad thing. Why would I ever ask any less of others than I ask of myself?"

"Well, in what world would it be appropriate for you to expect all people everywhere to be able to meet the same standards you've set for yourself?"

"In a world where everyone's exactly like me?" Robin smiled. "OK, I think I see where we're going with this. Basically, I'm assuming that because something is simple for me, it's simple for everyone, or at least *should* be. Like if I'm able to wake up at 4 a.m. every day, then everybody should be able to wake up at 4 a.m. every day."

"And not only do you think they should be *able* to, what else do you believe?"

"They should *want* to do it! And when they don't, I'm like, 'What's wrong with you?'"

We had another good laugh over that.

"Robin, can you see how every time you hold yourself up as *the* standard to meet and others miss the mark, it leads you down this slippery slope of frustration and negativity and criticism? Which leads to these 'losing your cool' moments?"

"I can definitely see that. Am I really that egotistical?"

"I'm not here to judge you one way or the other. What I can say is that this belief is getting in your way now. It's probably served you well in some capacity, or else it wouldn't be such a strong operating principle, as you called it. So, in what way do you think this assumption of 'If I can do it, so can you' has worked for you?"

"That's the thing that's really stumped me with this, Muriel. I feel like that principle is what's gotten me to where I am. There have been so many times in my career and even in my personal life where once I realized that I had it in me, that I was really capable, it gave me that extra push to keep going. Like I remember when I started my career in banking, and we'd be in these meetings where everyone was talking over each other and making their points, and I used to just sit back waiting until I had the perfect thing to say to speak up. Then one day I realized none of those guys were any smarter than I was. They may have acted like it, but they weren't. So why was I holding back? I was like, 'If they can do it, so can I,' and I did."

"So this belief motivated you."

"Yes! It did."

"And you thought the same thing would be motivating for others— if you could do it, they could too."

"Absolutely! But it's not just that. Look, I'm not like most of these people. I didn't have it easy coming up. I had to overcome a lot to get where I am. Not to get into the nitty-gritty of it all, but if my life were turned into a movie, it would be titled *Against All Odds*."

Robin went on to share some of the adversity she had to overcome. Unlike most of my clients, Robin came from a family that had actively tried to dissuade her from pursuing higher education. No one in her family had been to college, and Robin's parents were fourth-generation small farmers who simply didn't see the value of an expensive university degree if Robin or any of her siblings were to continue farming. Robin shared that she had caused her parents and grandparents considerable disappointment by choosing not to carry on the family tradition. Then, she had to find a way to finance her undergraduate and graduate degrees entirely on her own, which she did through a combination of scholarships and part-time jobs. From there, she launched a career in a field where relationships and connections with wealthy investors and donors were paramount. This was a world she was not accustomed to and in which she knew no one. She had to learn how to navigate it without the ease that familiarity lends, and build relationships from the ground up, without the benefit of being an insider.

"But I *made* it, Muriel," she said. "I had grit. I fought hard and I worked hard to not let anything get in my way. I climbed mountain after mountain to get here. And listen, I'm no one special. Just a kid who grew up on a small family farm, who wanted something different. So, yeah, at this point, it's hard for me to look at just about anything and think it's insurmountable. And I see no reason why anyone else can't do the same."

"I love your story. It's clearly motivated you, and you have a lot to be proud of," I said. "But it's *your* story. No one else's. If we stick with your metaphor, the fact that you can climb Mount Kilimanjaro doesn't necessarily mean I can or your coworker can or your boss can. In fact, on some days, even expert mountain climbers won't be able to make it to the summit."

Robin studied me for a moment. "I do see what you're saying," she said, "but there's still a part of me that believes 'With the right training and equipment and support, anybody can make it to the top.'"

"You're absolutely right," I said. "With all the right conditions in place—motivation, training, strength and stamina, mental fortitude, skill, the right equipment, adequate supplies, good weather, a capable

Potential Costs of This Hidden Blocker

Quiet and actual quitting: When employees aren't acknowledged or appreciated, they're not motivated to perform at their best. And if they're in a toxic work environment where leaders are never satisfied with their performance and engage in yelling, shaming, or harsh criticism when they fail to meet expectations, employees may withdraw and become disengaged as a form of self-protection and, ultimately, resign.

Poor work relationships and lack of trust: It's very difficult to work with someone who is always on the lookout for others' flaws and eager to point them out. Research shows that colleagues who expect perfection from others and are critical when they fail to achieve it (other-oriented perfectionism) are the least preferred type of colleague to work with, and the most likely to experience interpersonal and work-related conflicts with coworkers.[a]

Stifled creativity and innovation: Criticizing, shaming, and reprimanding others sabotages psychological safety, the sense that it is OK to pose questions, try novel ideas, make occasional mistakes, and take risks. In such a culture, employees tend to shut down and play it safe.

guide, and so on and so forth—it's very likely a climber will succeed. But it's never guaranteed. There are a thousand and one variables that have to be in place for that to happen, and every single person will come to this task with their own unique set of circumstances and variables, including disadvantages that aren't visible."

"You're saying I can't assume that because all the right variables were in place for me, they are for the other person. And that I can't assume everyone has what it takes to be able to do what *I* think is doable."

"Exactly. The issue isn't in your *desire* for them to climb the mountain. The issue is in your assumption that they have everything it takes

Higher risk of failure: Leaders who push others to do something that is beyond their competency or for which they're not prepared increase the likelihood of failure. Individual workers as well as the organization and those it serves end up paying the price.

Risk of unethical behavior: Organizational psychology has found that when leaders emphasize perfection and place unrealistic demands on their employees, it can create the perception that leaders want employees to engage in dubious behavior to meet those demands (for example, "Do whatever it takes"). With this perception in place, employees are more willing to relax their own moral code in order to meet the unreasonable demands placed on them.[b]

a. Emily Kleszewski and Kathleen Otto, "The Perfect Colleague? Multidimensional Perfectionism and Indicators of Social Disconnection in the Workplace," *Personality and Individual Differences* 162, no. 110016 (2020): https://doi.org/10.1016/j.paid.2020.110016.

b. Jiang Feng et al., "Why Does a Leader's Other-Oriented Perfectionism Lead Employees to Do Bad Things? Examining the Role of Moral Disengagement and Moral Identity," *Frontiers in Psychology* 15 (2024): https://doi.org/10.3389/fpsyg.2024.1290233.

to be able to do so, based on how you see *yourself*, not on them and their unique circumstances."

Robin nodded. "Bottom line, I need to stop expecting others to be able to do something just because I think I can. And I *definitely* need to stop losing my cool when they can't."

"No argument there," I said with a smile.

Though many people intend for this belief to be a motivator for others, especially those of us in Western societies who are conditioned to believe that we can do anything if we just work hard and persevere, it's easy to miss, as Robin did, that "if I can do it, so can you" can come across as the exact opposite of motivational. "Might this well-known expression be viewed as challenging, maybe even confrontational?" wonders retired clinical psychologist Leon Seltzer. "As in, 'If I can do it, shouldn't you be able to do it, too?' Or, 'If you *can't* do it, too, something must be wrong with you.'"[1] Much depends, of course, on the tone and attitude with which this expression is offered, and as we saw, Robin's tone was neither supportive nor motivational.

The Roots of This Hidden Blocker

Individuals with this hidden blocker have a strong tendency to believe their ideas, solutions, and perspective are superior to others'. Much of the time, they don't harbor this as a conscious thought, but if we peel back the onion, we'll likely find some version of "It's not me, it's you" at the heart of the "If I can do it, so can you" belief.

It's actually quite natural to believe that our particular take on things is both true and optimal. But if we encounter a perspective that's different—let's say a colleague comes up with a process that's not the same as ours but we recognize as valuable—most of us can adapt to their approach without much difficulty. People with this hidden blocker, however, have a hard time letting go of their way, which they take to be objective truth rather than subjective opinion, just one way among many.

Naive realism is the tendency to believe that our perceptions reflect an unbiased and unfiltered view of the world, and to assume that others share our view. Have you ever been incredulous that someone finds your favorite movie intolerable—or been astounded (and horrified) by *their* choice of favorite movie? That's a relatively harmless instance of naive realism. Of course, when the stakes are higher, so are the consequences. If we believe that our perspective is inherently superior, that means others' are inherently inferior, and it means we're closed off to others' perspectives, ideas, or solutions. The Decision Lab aptly calls naive realism "an egocentric cognitive distortion," one that leads us to ignore perceptions that conflict with our own. And that, in turn, "makes us miss out on an opportunity to expand our worldview."[2]

Another common root of this hidden blocker is plain old insecurity. Many times, someone who behaves with a lot of bluster and bravado is trying to mask or compensate for feelings of insecurity or low self-esteem. Their harsh judgment and criticism of those who fail to meet their high standards is actually a way of projecting the things they don't like about themselves onto other people.

Seen in this light, Robin's actions, while not excusable, make sense. In an attempt to assuage their feelings of insecurity and preserve their worth, other-oriented perfectionists like Robin deflect attention away from their own shortcomings and insecurities and project them onto others. Their inability to accept anything less than the best from *others* is actually their inability to accept anything less than the best from *themselves*. This hidden blocker insulates them not only from culpability, but more crucially for them, from the potential painful realization that they themselves are not up to par.

There are also external sources and influences behind this hidden blocker. If you grew up in an environment that accepted nothing less than perfection, you will naturally carry on those tendencies and apply them to yourself and others. The same happens if you grew up in an environment where people were highly evaluative in picking apart everything—how you or others dress, speak, look, act, and so on—especially if they were doing so under the guise of trying to help you. And if you turned out OK according to the exacting standards that were set for you, and some part of you believes those standards are *why* you turned out OK, why not do the same with others? These are learned behaviors that you will carry into your personal and professional life.

Years of societal conditioning also assure us that we can achieve anything if only we work hard enough, as we saw with Robin. This belief is a powerful and pervasive component of Western cultures, perhaps best encapsulated in "the American dream." But of course, while inspiring, it is both limited and limiting. In its overgeneralization, this belief results in misguided expectations and advice that can discourage individuals, when in spite of their best efforts, the outcome is not the dream they envisioned. And certainly, this overgeneralized belief fails to consider that the traditional American dream—hard work can overcome any barrier or disadvantage—does not apply equally to everyone. For every Robin who is able to succeed despite adversity, there are countless others who are denied equal access to opportunity by entrenched systemic forces such as racism and genderism, to name just a few, that are beyond their control. Bottom line, believing that everyone can accomplish what you did if they simply carry out the same actions misses the stark reality that circumstances and starting points are vastly different from person to person. As one commentator put it, "If I can do it, you can do it" would only ring true if we all had the same upbringing, the same life story, the same strengths and weaknesses, and the same wiring in our nervous systems.[3] And, might I add, the same luck.

I must admit that at one point, I also got caught up in this false narrative. When I launched a new venture, I was a quintessential rainmaker. I kicked it into high gear to build a client base, grow revenue, and expand the business all while writing a book, maintaining a full load of clients, and parenting two young children. It was difficult, but I did it, and I thought, *Wow, if I can do this, anybody can.*

Which wasn't so harmful as a private thought, but when a colleague wasn't delivering the same results as I was, alarm bells started going off for me. It didn't take long for my frustration to creep into our meetings. I kept pushing and prodding and reminding them of the goals that needed to be met, but always with the assurance that I knew they could do it. Because if I was able to do so much under tough circumstances, I was certain my colleague could too. I genuinely believed I was motivating this person.

One evening, I was sharing my frustrations with a good friend who's a successful business owner. "I don't get it!" I said. "If I can do all this, why can't they?"

My friend started laughing. "Girl!" she said. "I say this with so much love. But you do realize that you have an incredibly high capacity to get stuff done and make something out of nothing that most folks *don't* have, right? Stop thinking that everyone can do what you do. It's not fair."

This was one of those light bulb moments when suddenly things make sense. Unfortunately, the damage was already done with my teammate, and they left the business a short time later. Once they'd made that decision, they shared that they just didn't feel like they could contribute at the level we needed them to. In hindsight, by we, they meant me.

Looking back, I deeply regret how I approached those interactions with my teammate, and perhaps with others as well. It wasn't until my friend pointed out that I was assuming everyone was as capable as I was that I began to see how this belief was blocking me, and how it was negatively impacting my ability to connect and mentor others despite my ability to effectively coach my clients. I had very high expectations of my peers, but I didn't consider them high, because they were no different than what I expected of myself. But they were not always realistic because they did not reflect the person in front of me.

Leaders will have better outcomes by motivating their colleagues and team members around a goal, a dream, a mission, or an objective, and then meeting them *where they are* to determine what path will work best for them, with all their unique circumstances, skills, proclivities, and yes, blockers, to get there. Then, if despite their best efforts, a colleague or team member is unable to get there just yet, a leader's job is to see them for what they *are* capable of and help them figure out what to do next (for instance, recalibrate the goal, train them to reach it, or if necessary, switch roles) rather than project constant disappointment and criticism and think that will somehow get them closer to the goal. Research has shown that the most effective motivation comes not from criticism or even the promise of reward, but from positive work environments where people are given autonomy, supportive relationships, appreciation, and the opportunity to engage in meaningful work.[4]

Robin Unblocks from Her Hidden Blocker

Robin had recommitted to the idea of becoming CEO, and she was willing to do the work it would take to get there. But before taking action, she had to decide what kind of leader she wanted to be.

"I want to be seen as someone who is strategic, results-oriented, decisive, and clear," she said. "I want people to consider me a CEO they *want* to work with because they find me consistently trustworthy, motivating, and inspiring. I want them to trust that I do care about them, even if we may not agree on everything. I think of it like those before-and-after pictures. If the before picture is now, the caption would say, 'Wrecking Ball: impatient, harsh, and insensitive' in how I deal with staff. I'd hope the after-picture caption would say, 'Steady Hand: patient, even-keeled, and empathetic.'"

"I love it—so we've got 'Wrecking Ball Robin' and 'Steady Hand Robin.' Wrecking Ball Robin is the one who goes off when someone doesn't meet her expectations, who insists, 'If I can do this, why can't you?'"

Robin closed her eyes. It was clear she was reflecting deeply on something, so I just waited until she opened her eyes again, nearly a full minute later.

"I was questioning again if I can actually do this," she said, "if I can ever be the type of CEO this org needs. I hate to admit it, but I don't know if Steady Hand Robin has ever shown up at work. Or at least, it's been rare. And then I thought of my mom.

"She's one of the few, or maybe the only, who sees Steady Hand Robin. I wasn't always that person with her, not for a long time. But I am now. My mom has dementia. I had a hard time accepting her diagnosis, especially in the earliest stages. I just wanted her to be able to push through. I'd say, 'Mom, I forget things too. If you just set up reminders like I do, there wouldn't be a problem.' And she'd get so discouraged. I even got her a time management app, and you can guess how that worked out. I have so many examples like that, where I was pushing her and using me as the baseline for why she could do what I was asking her to do if she just tried hard enough. It's like I was assuming she didn't *want* to do more. I think that was easier for me to deal with than admitting she was actually not capable. It wasn't until I started really accepting where she was at—what she's capable of and what she's not—that I was able to ease up. That doesn't mean I don't encourage her to stay active and do things to keep her as healthy as possible, but I approach it differently. I'm more patient. I coach her through things rather than demand it. And I don't criticize her when she makes a mistake. So, yeah, Steady Hand Robin shows up with my mom these days."

"Let me ask you something," I said. "In those moments with your mom, what's the assumption you're making about her that allows you to show up as Steady Hand Robin?"

"That she's doing the best she can with what's at her disposal right now."

"And as a result of that?"

"I meet her where she is. I treat her the way *she* needs to be treated rather than how I think I would want to be treated."

"That's the platinum rule! Treat others the way *they* want to be treated rather than the golden rule of 'Treat others the way *you* would like to be treated.'[5] So walk me through how you can apply this with your staff. The next time someone doesn't meet your expectations, what's the assumption that will allow Steady Hand Robin to step up, rather than Wrecking Ball Robin?"

"I think instead of 'If I can do it, so can you,' what would be more helpful is 'You're doing the best you can at this moment.'"

"What will that accomplish?" I asked.

"Well, number one, I'm not making it about *me*, so there's a huge difference. It makes me start from a place of accepting the person for what they've done and where they are in that particular situation. Instead of resisting it and pushing back immediately. It's dealing with the reality of the situation—kind of like, 'It is what it is. Now what?'"

"What you're speaking of is equanimity. No matter what happens, you see the situation for what it is and respond as such. Because it's only when you see things clearly that you can make a discerning decision of what to do next. Wrecking Ball Robin doesn't see things clearly because she's projecting her own capabilities onto the other person. Steady Hand Robin sees the capabilities in front of her clearly and, from there, can decide what to do."

"So it's not about just doing nothing and letting things be," Robin said. "Because I think up until now, I thought if I didn't push, I was accepting mediocrity. But I don't think that's what you're saying. You're saying to accept the person's capabilities where they are when it comes to that specific deliverable . . . and then move to action to figure out how they can level up."

"Exactly. Let's talk about how you move others to action. Are you open to a suggestion? The next time someone doesn't deliver what you expect, don't react immediately. The first thing I want you to do is to name what's happening, but that's all. Don't make up a story about it. So, for example, with the comms director, naming it would be something like, 'There are some key points missing in the press release.' Telling yourself a story about it would be more like, 'I can't believe he messed up. What is *wrong* with him? Why can't he do something so basic?' Make sense so far?"

"Yes. Basically, leave out the narration. The commentary."

"Exactly. Focus on the task, not the person. Next, ask yourself if the reason they didn't deliver was because of a skill issue—they don't know how to—or a will issue—they don't want to. Or both. If you don't know which it is, then find out."[6]

"I could say something like, 'Could you walk me through your thinking on this press release? What do you think works well and what doesn't? What would you do differently next time?' Basically, questions that will give me more context before I respond."

"One hundred percent," I said. "You seek to understand by clarifying *context*, *intent*, and *actions*. CIA—that will help you remember. If you can get that intel, it will give you a better sense of whether he doesn't have the skill—in this case, maybe he's not experienced in writing partnership press releases, or he didn't understand what was expected, who knows? Or, maybe he didn't have the will—maybe he didn't want to revise it, which led to shortcomings. Or maybe he disregarded the importance of the release. The point is, we don't know, so we're just engaged in guesswork for now, which isn't helpful. Your job will be to get to the core of *why* what's happening is happening, and then you respond to *that*. You identify what's at the core for *him*—not you—that led to the omission. And then you address it."

"That's really interesting," Robin said. "I like that. And I think it's actually what Diane does. When issues come up, she definitely deals with problems head-on. But she's never hard on the person, even when they've had a performance failure. Even with me. She's called me out, but never in public, and she's never belittled me. She asks me questions and tries to understand my end of it, but she's very clear about what she expects of me going forward and she does it all without losing her cool. Now, whether I've taken heed or not is a different story. But as I'm saying all this out loud, I can see how critical a piece that is in the culture we have, and why folks love working for her.

"When Diane leaves, there's the risk that the culture leaves with her. And no one wants to see that happen because what motivates people the most here is the mission and the culture. So I see the importance of the next CEO needing to be a culture carrier. It's really not about me; it's about the heart and soul of this organization. And if I want to lead it, I need to make it part of my way of leading as well."

"Well said, Robin."

I went on to coach Robin on and off for a few years, all the way up to her selection as the next CEO, and when she transitioned into the new role. In terms of her goal to not be as hard on people as she'd been in the past, hers was not a linear path by any means. There was some backsliding, but she stayed committed and learned every time. What made a big difference in her progress was her ability to acknowledge and show remorse when she slid back into her wrecking-ball ways. By not putting herself on a pedestal and being vulnerable enough to show that she too made mistakes, it gave her greater latitude to be more accepting of others when they fell short.

Would Robin ever win the prize for being the most empathetic, warm, and fuzzy leader? Probably not. But the effort she put into being Steady Hand Robin paid dividends. A year after she became CEO, I gathered feedback on her, all of which showed a positive direction from where she started. One comment in particular encapsulated the sentiment about Robin's journey:

> *Robin has done a great job with moving into the CEO role. It has been not only a personal transition for her; she is also transitioning the organization out of a founder-led model and into a new era. I give her very high marks for how she's handling all of this. She's improved tremendously in how she responds to others, and you can see her checking herself. She still drives for results, but she also seems to value others more now to get to those results.*

During our final meeting, after reviewing some lessons learned from her first year on the job, Robin closed with this: "I stopped making it about me all the time. And when I did that, I got out of my own way."

Coach Yourself

Many successful people tend to believe that what works for them works for everyone else—that if you do what they do, you too will be just as successful. While this belief can inspire, it cannot be applied as a universal rule. Instead, we should consider extending Marshall Goldsmith's often-quoted book title and mantra "What got you here won't get you there" to "What got you here won't always get others there." For example, some leaders believe that if they work really, really hard, they can overcome anything—and that if they can do that, others can too. But as we saw with Robin, it's never that simple.

Do you think you share Robin's hidden blocker of "If I can do it, so can you"? What assumptions do you hold about yourself that you automatically believe to be true for others? Name the way this belief shows up for you, and then identify a reframed belief that loosens the grip of this hidden blocker. Then let your reframed belief inspire actions that will help you sustain an unblocked state in which you meet others where they are, rather than from your position.

From Blocked

- If I can do it, so can you.

- I wouldn't ask anyone to do anything I wouldn't do.

- I don't expect any more or less of you than I do of myself.

- I treat others the way I want to be treated.

- If I could make it work, there's no reason you can't.

- I've done it, which shows it can be done.

- I figured it out, so there's really no excuse for you.

To Unblocked

- What worked for me might not work for everyone.

- I will treat others the way they want or need to be treated.

- Everyone is doing the best they can with what they have at their disposal.

- Everyone has their own strengths and challenges, so we may need to approach this differently.

- I will meet people where they're at and adapt from there.

- I managed to do it, but I understand that everyone's situation is different.

- We all have different starting points, so I know it might be harder for some.

To Action

- *Focus on the task, not the person.* Calibrate your expectations of others against their level of skill and will relative to the situation and task at hand.

- *Assess without comparing.* Focus on assessing someone's capability or commitment without mentally comparing them to your own path or outcomes.

- *Check your assumptions of what you label as "easy" or "difficult" for others.* Remind yourself that something that may feel simple for you might be complex for someone else, and vice versa.

- *Seek input on how you can support them.* Ask others if there are specific ways you can encourage or assist them, respecting their pace and approach. Ask questions like, "What do you think would work best for you?" rather than suggesting your own method.

Chapter 8

I Can't Say No

You can have it all. Just not all at once.

—OPRAH WINFREY

Matt was a senior manager at a top-tier management consulting firm with an "up or out" tenure policy. A rigorous and competitive system, employees had to earn promotions within an expected time frame or leave. Underperforming employees usually left on their own rather than face the possibility of being pushed out. As a result, only a small number made it to the top echelons of the firm.

Matt had succeeded so far, having been promoted to senior manager a few years ago. Now there was only one level left—associate partner—before he'd reach his ultimate goal of becoming a full partner.

I'd met Matt over the course of working with other partners at the firm, including Robert, who'd become his mentor. Robert was a huge supporter, so I was surprised when he texted to ask if we could chat as soon as possible, as there was "a big issue" with Matt.

"Thanks for making yourself available on short notice," Robert said. "I know we don't have a ton of time, so I'll get right to it. Matt is up for promotion to associate partner at the end of the year, but based on what I'm hearing, I don't think he's going to make it."

"Oh no," I said. "Does he have any idea?"

"He does," Robert said. "I met with him yesterday and gave him a heads-up. I didn't want him to feel blindsided, and you know how we operate here—it's always best for folks to know where they stand so they know how to move forward."

"How'd he take the news?"

"Not well, to put it mildly. He didn't say much, but he was visibly upset. He did ask if this meant he'd never get promoted, or just not this year. I told him that given this was his first time up for associate partner and the partners seemed to be on the fence about him, this was more a signal that he has some things he needs to work on to get promoted in the next round. That's when your name came up. I shared how helpful you'd been to me when I was on the partner track and that maybe he should consider working with an executive coach. He said he'd welcome the support and is game to work with you, if you are."

I offered to follow up with Matt. I wanted to make sure this was something he actually wanted to do and not something he'd agreed to just because it was suggested. In the meantime, Robert said he'd talk to a few of the partners and get some more specific feedback for Matt.

Matt called me the next day. "I knew it couldn't be good when Robert asked me for a sit-down," he said. "But I was totally blindsided by what he said. How is it possible I didn't see this coming? All I've been thinking since is, has the goalpost moved?"

"I get it. Where are you now with all this?"

"To be honest, I've been vacillating between saying, 'Screw them. I'll just go somewhere I'm wanted,' or refusing to give up. I mean, I've built my entire career here, and I really do like this firm and the people. Plus, Robert did emphasize that not getting the promotion the first time doesn't mean I'm out of the running forever. So there's a part of me that doesn't want to miss the chance of trying again next year. But I also don't want to be strung along. I'm torn."

"Understandable," I said. "If you stay, what would you need to make it work for you?"

"I'd want to make sure I'm working on the right things to help me get promoted," Matt said. "I *thought* I was, but given what just happened, I clearly don't know. I guess that's how your coaching could help. I don't know what I don't know."

"OK, so listen," I said. "I think right now what you *do* know is that you're not sure whether to give it another shot or take your efforts elsewhere. I'd recommend you just sit with the decision for now, listen to your gut, and let that guide your next step. Let it marinate over the weekend. Then ping me next week and let me know what you want to do. Either way, you'll be OK."

The following Monday morning, I got a text from Matt: "Going to give it another shot. Will let Robert know that I want to work with you. More soon."

Matt Uncovers His Hidden Blocker

A few weeks later, Matt and I sat down with Robert to get aligned around his developmental goals. Robert had followed through on his promise to get more nuanced feedback from the partners for Matt and was ready to share.

"From what I'm gathering, there's high performance and there's baseline performance," Robert said. "Matt is viewed as playing the baseline—enough to be in the game but not enough to get him over the hump from senior manager to associate partner."

He turned to face Matt. "I think there are three categories where you need to make some visible shifts that would put you in a stronger position to get promoted next round."

Robert wrote them out on a sheet of paper and slid it across the table to Matt (see table 8-1).

"Let me start with client impact," he said. "You've got a stellar reputation for coming through for clients. The partners know this.

TABLE 8-1

Matt's path to promotion

	From baseline	To high performance
Client	Project execution	Trusted adviser
Team	Task focused	Impact focused
Firm	Passenger's seat	Driver's seat

The clients know this. They know if you're on the engagement, the work's going to get done. The issue is that while you're definitely in demand, you're not the go-to for client executives when they want a sounding board or strategic perspective. And that's a huge indicator of your future ability to generate business, which as you know is critical as an associate partner.

"The second issue is how you engage with your project teams. Your teams love you and want to work with you, and your project after-action review scores with your teams are off the charts. There's a question about whether you're getting the most out of them, though. Your utilization rate is actually *too* high, which signals that you're doing a lot of the work yourself and not leveraging your team effectively. That's going to be really important as your project load increases in scope and complexity as an associate partner, so that was a big red flag.

"Last, there's your firm presence. The partners know you, but they don't *know you* know you. They see you as a great foot soldier but not necessarily as a peer, and the closer you get to becoming a partner, the more they need to see you as someone who can sit at the table with them. The only way that happens is if they get to know you and see you in action."

Matt had been voraciously taking notes as Robert spoke. But I could tell that it was also a way of keeping his emotions in check. The sting about not getting promoted was fresh, and Robert's feedback was bringing it back up.

I thanked Robert and told him I thought it would be helpful if Matt and I had a chance to debrief before we came back with a plan. "I also may follow up with some of the folks you spoke to just to get more context, if that's OK with you."

"Of course," Robert said. "And, Matt, I know this is a lot, but everyone knows you're capable, and the sooner you can move the needle, the better. I'm here to help."

With that, Robert left the room.

I gave Matt a moment to gather his thoughts. "How's all this landing with you?" I asked. "Does anything resonate?"

"I still can't believe how much I was missing the mark," Matt said. "It's like this whole time I thought I was supposed to be doing *ABC* to get promoted, and somehow I missed the memo that I was actually supposed to be doing *XYZ*. I thought I was doing fine. Great, even."

"Why did you think that?"

"Because, as Robert said, it's not like I haven't been in demand. I'm always staffed on projects. Partners negotiate with each other to figure out who gets me as senior manager, and clients personally request me all the time. And whatever they want, I come through. But then did you hear what he said? I've actually been doing so many things that it's a red flag for them. I thought all that pointed to the fact that I was a high performer—not just baseline."

"A high performer relative to what?" I asked.

Matt gave me a long look, thinking. "I'm a high performer as a senior manager. But not shining bright enough for them to believe I can be a high-performing associate partner."

"I think that's it," I said. "I don't think the goalpost has changed. You're knocking it out of the park when it comes to your current role, but not doing enough in their eyes to demonstrate your future potential for the next level. Relative to your peers who will get promoted this round, the partners haven't seen enough evidence to place a bet on promoting you just yet."

Signs You May Have This Hidden Blocker

What you may see and feel

You say yes even though your inner voice says, "There's no way I can take on another thing."

You have a genuine desire to help others. You go out of your way to make sure they don't have to carry the burden of extra work.

You say yes to things to avoid the discomfort of saying no. Even the thought of saying no causes you mental or physical distress (excessive worry, guilt, shame, a knot in your stomach, tightness in your chest, and so on).

You avoid upsetting or disappointing others, even if it's at your own expense.

You procrastinate on responding or avoid someone because you don't want to turn them down. You overthink whether or how to say no.

What others may see and feel

You are the go-to person to get things done.

You are selfless, tireless, one who will take one for the team, and always willing to help.

You rarely, if ever, question or decline a request to do something.

You are a doer but not necessarily a leader.

"But how am I supposed to do everything Robert mentioned?" Matt said. "They're constantly lobbing things my way. So, realistically, when am I supposed to find the time to meet with clients more than I already am or go golfing with the senior partners so they can *'know me* know me'? It's just not fair. I bet you that Adam, one of the guys I started with, will get promoted. Case in point, just last week during one of our busiest times, Adam went to dinner with a senior partner while I was left behind to make sure the client presentation was ready. As they were walking out the door, Adam turned around and was like, 'You good? Text me if you need anything.' And that's it! That wasn't the first time, either. They all do this to me."

"What did you do after Adam left?"

"What was I supposed to do? I stayed and finished the presentation. It's not like I could say no."

"You couldn't? Adam did."

"Because he knew I'd say yes and stay. So that's the way it is—*I can't say no.*"

Matt Unpacks His Hidden Blocker

It was clear that Matt felt he had no choice but to respond with a *yes* to all the demands placed on him—the demands that kept him so busy being a high-performing senior manager that he had no time or energy to build and demonstrate his muscles as an associate partner. It's difficult for anyone to accept any responsibility for what's holding them back if they feel they don't have a choice in the matter. Without a sense of agency, Matt would not see this issue as something that was within his power to change, but rather as something that *others* needed to change. While change on both sides is ideal, the only thing one can control is their own beliefs and behaviors—not that of others. I asked Matt what he felt he couldn't say no to.

"Basically everything," he said. "The partners, Robert included, are always asking me to take another project or support them on a client deliverable. And I always do it. What I'm realizing is that I'm being penalized for *their* actions. Why can't they just stop asking me to take care of so many things? Then maybe I'd actually be able to finish what's on my own list and pay attention to relationship-building and everything else Robert mentioned."

"Is that what you're waiting for? For them to stop asking so much of you?"

"I mean . . . is that too much to expect?"

"Maybe it shouldn't be, but do you think they ever will?"

"In all likelihood, no."

"So how long are you willing to wait for them to change? And how much is their behavior under your control?" I asked.

Matt frowned.

"Look, I'm not absolving them of what they're doing," I said. "Not at all. But I'm far more interested in how *you* respond to their behavior in a way that serves you and helps you meet your goal to get promoted. So, the way I see it is you have four options: (1) keep doing what you're doing, (2) wait for them to change their behavior, (3) change your response to their behavior and see what happens, or (4) leave altogether.[1] Since you've decided to stay, let's cross number four off the list. So which door would you like to walk through— one, two, or three?"

"I don't really love any of these choices," Matt said. "But option one is a nonstarter because it will basically land me exactly where I am. Option two is very appealing, but it will likely frustrate me to no end because it's probably not even possible. I'm not willing to bet my future on that. So option three it is. I guess I need to respond differently."

"In what way exactly?"

"Saying no more often or at all, for starters."

"And what will that require of you?"

"To just do it—just say no."

Matt was ready to jump straight to action, as many of us would be. It can be so energizing to feel you can finally see your way through a tough situation, and leaders who are accustomed to problem-solving and executing quickly are always primed for action. I was curious to see if Matt's newfound enthusiasm to turn down requests would actually come to fruition. At our next meeting, I asked Matt how it had gone the past few weeks.

"It didn't," Matt said. "Like at all."

"Ten points for honesty," I said. "OK, so if saying no didn't happen, what did?"

"Same old stuff as before," he said. "Someone threw a ball at me, and I caught it and ran with it instead of letting it drop or throwing it back to them or to someone else. Even worse is that in the past, I wasn't even aware I was doing this. Now I'm fully aware that I should be saying no, but I don't. And I'm beating myself up over that."

I often have to explain to my clients that just because they've decided to think about something differently and they really want to change things, it doesn't mean they can flip the switch and, voilà, it happens right away. As the saying goes, many things are easier said than done, even for high achievers like Matt.

A model I've found useful when it comes to learning something new is the conscious competence model. It's depicted in various forms, but my favorite, the Conscious Competence Ladder, is pictured in figure 8-1.[2] It's helpful to understand our thoughts and feelings as we pick up a new belief or learn a new skill, and to stay motivated and manage self-expectations throughout the learning curve.

I sketched out the Conscious Competence Ladder for Matt and pointed to the unconscious incompetence step. "Look, you were here—you didn't know what you didn't know. But now you're aware of what you should do—that's conscious incompetence—and even if you're not doing it yet, this is a good thing. So there's no need to beat yourself up. It means that even though you may not have gotten to a place where you can say no in the moment, you're on the path to learning it."

"But either way, I'm incompetent," Matt said, laughing. "Thanks a lot!"

"Oh, but you're *conscious* about it, which is a lot further than you were a few weeks ago," I said, laughing with him. "This part is necessary to pave the way for what comes next, which is conscious competence—that is where you know how to say no and you're confident in your ability to do it. That's golden, because that's when you

FIGURE 8-1

Conscious Competence Ladder

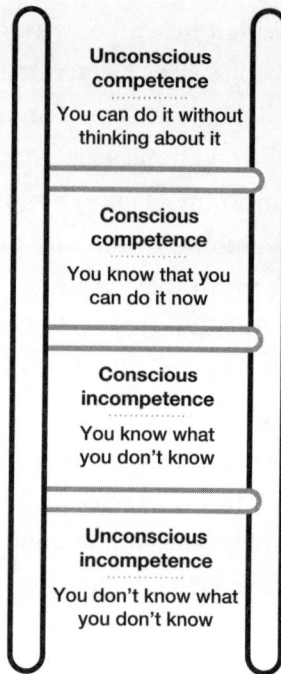

Unconscious competence
You can do it without thinking about it

Conscious competence
You know that you can do it now

Conscious incompetence
You know what you don't know

Unconscious incompetence
You don't know what you don't know

can make a choice whether to say yes or no. That's what we're aiming for."

"Alright, how do I get there?"

"With some practice . . . and some patience," I said with a smile. "You're now trying to learn to say no more often. Which means that somewhere along the line, you learned *not* to say no. You've learned to say yes so well that you don't even realize you're doing it. So, how'd you learn to say yes so often? Who taught you that?"

"I don't know if I can identify one particular person or thing that taught me that saying yes was good and saying no was bad. I guess it's always been part of my DNA."

Matt described playing competitive tennis growing up. He shared how his dad had drilled into him that no matter how good you were, there was always another player who was willing to do another hour on the court, another tournament, another workout. Climbing the rankings meant saying yes as much as possible or someone else would take your place. Now work felt the same for Matt.

"When I first joined the firm, I saw how the associates who didn't take the assignments when they were asked found themselves on the bench, unstaffed," he said. "Every one of those people ended up leaving. I didn't want that to be me, so if a partner asked, I did it. I think that's why Robert took me under his wing. He knew he could rely on me, and I became his go-to."

"So, in order to stay ahead of the pack, you felt you needed to say yes to what was being asked of you. And that's stayed with you until now?"

"Yeah, it has. There's a part of me that's concerned that if I say no, I'll get penalized."

"Is that what holds you back from saying no more often?"

"As I say it out loud, yes. Especially in this up-or-out culture." Matt paused. "But there's something else too," he went on. "I get really uncomfortable having to say no to folks. Like just thinking about it now puts my stomach in knots. I'm concerned people will get upset or it will be awkward and uncomfortable between us. I guess it's just easier for me to say yes, because then I won't have to deal with any of the negative fallout from the alternative."

"Is this just with the partners and clients?"

"No, it's pretty much everybody. When we get more work, I don't want to make my team feel overworked, so I just do it myself. I don't want to have to say no to them in terms of how they want to spend their time. And, yeah, same in my personal life—my sister drops by all the time to use my home gym and most times I want to tell her no, but it's easier to just let her use it than to have that conversation."

"I think you've just gotten to the root of it," I said. "It's not just a matter of you learning how to say no. It's about understanding that your default of 'I can't say no' has played a really powerful role in your life—it's helped you stay at the top of your game for a very long time, and it's helped you stay feeling connected with people you

Potential Costs of This Hidden Blocker

Exhaustion and eventual burnout: As leaders take on more, others assume they're capable of extra and rely on them to do more. A vicious cycle ensues, putting leaders at risk for exhaustion, overwork, and eventually, burnout, as they're never able to recover from work-related stress.

Exploitation: There is evidence that workers who've made a habit of saying yes are at risk for being taken advantage of. Research from Duke University shows that passionate employees "are more likely to get asked to do unpaid work, work on the weekends, and handle tasks that are not a part of their roles. This tendency springs from two beliefs: that passionate employees would have volunteered to do the extra work anyway, and that extra work is its own reward for someone who loves their job."[a]

Lack of advancement: Saying yes indiscriminately and becoming overcommitted means leaders lose the capacity to invest in opportunities to position themselves for advancement. Spread too thin, critical advancement factors such as taking time for strategic thinking, cultivating relationships with key stakeholders, or building an external-facing presence fall by the wayside.

Resentment: As the pile-on continues, it's easy to become resentful about being overburdened, about no one recognizing how these leaders routinely go above and beyond, and how no one will step in to give them a break. Disappointment and cynicism can set in as they fail to achieve their own goals.

a. Dina Denham Smith, "How (and When) to Say No to the Boss," hbr.org, May 10, 2021, https://hbr.org/2021/05/how-and-when-to-say-no-to-the-boss.

deem important even if it meant putting your own needs aside. But it's given you a false sense of comfort; until now, it's probably taken you less energy to grin and bear it than to assert yourself and say no when people ask you to do things."

"Yeah. It's definitely been helpful to me. But now it's clearly not."

The Roots of This Hidden Blocker

Dealing with this hidden blocker can be tricky because serving others can be so rewarding. And let's face it, most people love having someone around who says yes all the time. I know this all too well, and I've done enough self-work to know where my own drive to say yes comes from. I come from a family where acts of service were the love language of choice. While it made us very giving and instilled a genuine desire to help others, at times it created a false sense of closeness based on obligation rather than true connection.

Not surprisingly, I carried this pattern into my adult life, both personally and professionally. My belief was that if I came through for others and said yes to their requests, even when it wasn't what I wanted or it wasn't aligned with my goals, things would work out because they'd come through for me when I needed them to. Or at least that was the story I told myself. It wasn't until I went through some painful experiences when that belief did not prove true that I started questioning it. I went out of my way to help others reach their goals and yet when it was my turn, they didn't help me. I said yes to decisions I didn't agree with to appease colleagues, and they still did what best served them without regard for my interests. I said yes to numerous work projects, only to feel resentful and overextended once the work got started. Throughout each of these experiences, I'd been waiting for others to reciprocate and start saying yes to me.

It took many, many times around this same block before I realized the onus was on me to break the pattern and advocate for myself. I realized that the main reason I said yes to so many demands was because I didn't want to face the discomfort of disappointing others and the guilt that would accompany it. Like Matt, I didn't want anyone to "feel bad," and as a result I opted to make myself feel bad instead. Ultimately, I realized that if I didn't expand my mindset from "I can't say no," I'd forever be caught in the false pretense that I had to put others' needs above my own to succeed.

Growing up in a family or community that expects you to be self-less and prioritize the needs of others is a common reason people develop the belief that they can't say no. And if you were reprimanded for talking back when you disagreed with the group, or if saying no was tantamount to disloyalty or shirking your duty, the belief can be even more entrenched. Similarly, growing up in an enmeshed family, where being close means having no boundaries and children are responsible for the happiness, self-worth, and well-being of their adult caregivers, can also easily give rise to the belief that you can't say no. Indeed, saying no in either of these scenarios carries a real risk of exclusion or rejection. The individual who dares buck the system—by insisting on healthy boundaries, prioritizing their own needs and goals, or declining a request—can be left with feelings of guilt, shame, and a diminishment of their own self-worth, which was built on the scaffolding of pleasing others and meeting their needs.[3]

It's also worth remembering that even if you were lucky enough to be born into the most loving and well-adjusted of families, it can still be difficult to say no. Many people are deeply conflict averse, and all of us have a primal desire to be liked and included. If we fear that saying no will cause tension or displeasure, will hurt someone's feelings or disappoint them, or will make us seem rude, selfish, or difficult, we will say yes rather than risk hurting others or potentially jeopardizing our place in the group. Research has shown that our need to be included is so strong that many people will agree to do things they don't want to do or even consider unethical to avoid the risk of displeasing others.[4] At root, these fears boil down to our primal fear of not belonging. Our brains are wired to avoid anything that has the potential to ostracize us from the group, because back in our evolutionary history, not belonging meant a loss of resources and safety. It's no wonder that saying no can feel like a risk not worth taking.

There are also fears that are specific to our work context that give rise to this hidden blocker. For example, you may fear that saying no will put your job at risk, that you'll be labeled as someone who isn't a team player, that you'll be replaced or outperformed by someone who will say yes, that you'll be overlooked for recognition, assignments, or promotions, that saying no will be interpreted as your inability to complete the task, that the opportunity won't come up again, or that saying no will harm a relationship with a colleague or your boss. None of these fears is surprising, given that society, and work culture especially, tells us that we get ahead by saying yes—and that saying no means we'll lose the traction we've gained.

Then, sometimes, saying yes when we want to say no comes down to a simple matter of expediency. You want to get back to what you were doing, you want to get out of a conversation, or you don't want to explain why you said no, so it's just easier and quicker to say yes and deal with the consequences later. And of course, plenty of people habitually say yes out of a genuine desire to help or because they're passionate about their organization's mission.

Just don't forget, advises clinical psychologist Emily Anhalt, that "your ability to accommodate others isn't an endless well."[5] Whatever the source of this hidden blocker and whatever continues to reinforce it, those who can't say no will eventually hit a wall. Maybe they're stretched so thin that their performance suffers, or they're unable to scale, or they miss out on a desirable opportunity because they're already overextended, or they're simply exhausted from doing too many things.

Or maybe, like Matt and me, they faced painful consequences from this belief and realize they need to do something different. They need to not only say no more often but start saying yes more judiciously, according to their strategic goals.

For me, saying no is still a constant practice. Hidden blockers can be deeply ingrained and never completely leave you. But if you can become aware of them and how they're preventing you from reaching your goals—and respond differently when they try to take over—it makes all the difference in how you lead.

Matt Unblocks from His Hidden Blocker

When Matt began to see and accept how the belief of "I can't say no" was getting in the way of reaching his career goals, and how it was playing out in other areas of his life as well, he was ready to figure out what he could do differently. That was the topic for our next meeting.

Matt admitted that he'd been struggling. "I actually started making a list of all the things I should start saying no to, and I just started to feel *really* uncomfortable and talked myself out of it. I stopped the list. It's like something is not letting me say no to the very things that are getting in my way. I don't know what it is."

"You don't?"

"Well, I know it's *me* . . . or at least, some part of me that isn't working in my own favor."

"That's right," I said. "It's not all of you. It's a part of you. One belief. And it's the belief that's been running you—and you've been letting it. It's been your CEO for a long time. You don't have to fire it altogether, because all the parts serve some purpose, but maybe now it's time to assign it to another role and promote another belief to that position. One that will be more supportive of you saying no to the activities that are holding you back."

These ideas are based on Richard Schwartz's internal family systems model, which says that each of us is made up of different subpersonalities, or "parts." None of the parts are bad, and in fact, every one of them serves an important purpose at different points in our lives. But these parts can sometimes be in conflict with each other, and sometimes, as Matt was experiencing, a part will come to the fore that isn't the best leader for the current context. The goal is never to eliminate any of the different parts of our personalities, but to help each one perform optimally and harmoniously with the others.[6]

"OK, so I'm not getting rid of that part altogether," said Matt. "That makes me more confident, because I can't suddenly become this person that goes from 'I can't say no' to 'I have to say no all the time.'

I like the notion that it's OK to say no sometimes and let that lead me. That would give me permission to be more discerning about what I say yes or no to. I can actually feel myself getting a little more relaxed as I think about it this way. It doesn't have to be all or nothing."

"I love that you're feeling more relaxed with this," I said. "That's a sign you're moving in the right direction. If you reframe it to 'It's OK to say no sometimes,' what do you think you'll say yes or no to?"

"That's the problem," said Matt. "I don't really trust my judgment on that just yet. I kind of need a checklist, or a decision tree, or something to help me. You know me, I'm a consultant, so I need a framework for everything."

"Alright, let's come up with a checklist," I said, "something you'll use as a filter to help you decide whether to say yes or no. Let's start with the things you think you need to consider in determining whether it's a yes-or-no response. And if I may, I'd like to add a third option, which is 'let's negotiate.' That's for the times when a straight-up yes or no isn't what's warranted, but there's another solution."

"I like that. OK, so I think I need to consider first and foremost if this is something that will get me closer to my goal of being promoted. Basically, what's in it for me? Because clearly that's where I've missed the mark. I've been focused on what's in it for everyone else and not what's going to get me closer to my own goal."

"Bingo," I said. "*Your* goals will always be a reliable guide, and focusing on what's in it for you is a great starting point. That will require you to be crystal-clear on the things that will get you closer to the goal of becoming an associate partner."

"Robert's feedback definitely gave me some clarity on that," Matt said. "I'd say the main goalposts are, one, being more visible to other partners as the front person and a peer rather than the backup; two, building a more advisory relationship with senior clients rather than execution; and three, developing and leveraging my project team instead of doing the work for them. If I do those three things consistently, I think it will get me closer to the uber-goal. So, if something checks any of those three things, and better yet all three, the answer is yes."

"Excellent. And if something comes your way that doesn't check any of those boxes?"

"Well, I know the right answer is to say no, but I'm still not sure if that's possible."

"OK, let's imagine it," I said. "What could you do instead of just immediately saying yes? Let's think of an example."

"Here's one," Matt said. "Robert wants me to finish up a presentation because he's under a time crunch and he doesn't trust his other senior manager to do it. Which by the way is a real situation that just happened that I said yes to and ended up missing another partner dinner."

"If you had a do-over with the 'I can say no sometimes' belief leading the way, what could you have done differently?"

"First, I'd check to see if I had the bandwidth to fulfill his request. If I did and I truly wasn't giving up something that was more aligned with my goals, then I'd do it. But if I didn't have the bandwidth, which in this case I really didn't because of the partner dinner, I'd have to say 'No,' 'Yes, but it's not going to get done tonight,' or 'Yes, but I can only spend an hour on it, so I'm happy to mark it up and give your manager direction so he can finish it up.'"

"And how would that have felt?"

"Uncomfortable, I'm sure, because it's not what I'm used to and also not what Robert's used to, but on the other side of it, it would have felt like I did right by both of us."

"I think you've seen saying no or yes as a zero-sum game, with no room for win-win situations. But most of the time, it's not about getting a win-win; it's about getting a win-some/win-some, where both you and the other person get 80 percent of what you want versus the full 100."[7]

"Yup. I think that's it," Matt said. "Until now, I felt like if others win, then I win. But in reality, I was losing and they were winning. If I do this win-some/win-some approach, I'd be able to work more aligned with my goals while helping others meet theirs."

Matt had one hesitation though. This approach meant there would be times he'd have to say no, flat out. He wondered how he could do that in a way that wouldn't seem harsh.

"You can and should be considerate of others' feelings," I said, "but you cannot control how they feel. So let me ask *you* a question. How can you say no without being harsh?"

"Well, context always helps. In Robert's case, I'll sit down with him and explain that to meet the expectations he's laid out for me, I'm going to have to say no to some of the things he throws at me or delegate to my team. That may soften the landing. He'll see that he's got some skin in this game too. And to be honest, I never turn my team down or ask them to help me out, so they'll probably see this as a breath of fresh air. Still, I think giving them a heads-up will help."

"What you're suggesting for yourself is managing expectations," I said. "And yes, that always helps. You are changing your behavior, and you're right, people won't be used to your new behavior, so it's best if you give them some context for what's coming. But, Matt, you've built so much equity in saying yes all these years that you've earned some leeway in saying no sometimes. Try not to overestimate how upset folks will get when you start saying no. Those fears are usually exaggerated."

Over the next few months, Matt put his plan to work. He used the checklist to help discern what to say yes or no to. He also used his work calendar and to-do lists to calibrate whether 80 percent of what he was engaged in was aligned with his professional goals. If it wasn't, he went through the process to determine if there were some "no" or "let's negotiate" opportunities he'd overlooked. These questions helped him clarify what needed to come to the forefront:

- If I had a completely free calendar to work toward my associate partner goal, how would I spend my time?

- Is there something I should be doing that I'm not because I'm too busy?

- Are there people I need to connect with but I haven't because I'm too busy?

Matt also enlisted the support of his team, his executive assistant, and Robert to help him stay aligned to this new way of operating. By making them part of the process, they were more apt to challenge him when he took something on that he didn't need to.

At the end of Matt's coaching engagement, I had a closing meeting with both Matt and Robert. Matt said the most surprising effect of basing his responses on his own goals was the improved relationships at work: by declining to take on so many things himself and instead let his team perform, there was greater trust among them, and by saying yes to more work-related social opportunities, Matt was enjoying getting to know the partners better. But probably the biggest growth for him was the comfort level he gained in being able to assert what he needed to be successful. With practice, Matt said, it became a little easier each time. Robert, meanwhile, reported that Matt had made huge strides, and based on what he was seeing as well as what he was hearing from others, he had confidence Matt was well positioned to be promoted at the next round.

Coach Yourself

Saying no is about setting a boundary and advocating for yourself. In the words of writer and therapist Prentis Hemphill, "Boundaries are the distance at which I can love you and me simultaneously."[8] In other words, you can have boundaries that serve you and the other even if it means not doing as they asked. But setting those boundaries requires being clear about what matters most to you and then acting accordingly. As we saw with Matt, the key to saying no at work is to set boundaries in a way that is authentic to you, preserves your key relationships, and supports your personal and professional goals, while at the same time adding value in your role. If you think the "I can't say no" hidden blocker is currently holding you back, begin by identifying how this specific belief shows up for you and naming it. Then, take your belief and reframe it in a way that preserves your boundaries and supports your goals.

From Blocked

- I can't say no.

- I have to say yes.

- I can't turn them down.

- No one else can do it but me.

- It's my job to say yes.

- If I don't do it, no one will.

- I don't want to burden anyone.

To Unblocked

- I can say no to some things.

- I can say no and still be supportive.

- I am allowed to consider my needs and priorities before making commitments to others.

- I will agree to do things that align with my goals and values, not to gain the acceptance of others.

To Action

- *Pause before responding to requests.* Assess your availability and priorities before agreeing, which prevents automatic yesses. Make sure you aren't saying yes out of guilt, fear, or conflict aversion.

- *Prepare and practice polite, direct ways to say no.* Having phrases ready, like "I'm unable to commit right now" or

"I have to prioritize my current obligations," can make it easier to decline. Clearly but kindly explain your limits without overapologizing or justifying, reinforcing that your boundaries are valid.

- *Reflect on positive outcomes.* After declining a request, take note of any benefits to reinforce the positive effects of setting limits.

Chapter 9

I Don't Belong Here

Our sense of belonging can never be greater than our
level of self-acceptance.

—BRENÉ BROWN

Adrian was the new chief strategy officer (CSO) for a *Fortune* 500 company after four years as the vice president of strategy within one of its divisions. He was promoted to head up strategy for the entire enterprise when the former CSO, Amanda, rotated out to become president for one of the company's major lines of business. The CSO role was coveted for this very reason. It was often a rite of passage for those who were seen as having high potential to eventually run a business, as well as a potential succession path for CEO.

Along with the other functional C-suite leads and the business presidents, Adrian was now reporting directly to Martin, the CEO. This meant that the company's senior leadership team (SLT), including Amanda's and Adrian's former boss Jim, one of the presidents, were now all his peers.

I had previously worked with other C-suite leaders at this company because the CEO was a big supporter of coaching and required all his direct reports to retain an executive coach when they joined his leadership team. In my initial conversation with Adrian, I found him open to receiving coaching support and thoughtful about the first six months in his new role.

"These past few months have been really interesting on a number of fronts," he said. "I've had to come in and assess the way we lead the strategic planning process for the entire company, which has been great because there's a lot of opportunity for improvement. I'm excited to move the needle there. I think the most eye-opening part, though, has been having to acclimate to the tenth floor."

The tenth floor was the top level of the company's headquarters where Adrian relocated after moving cross-country to take on his new job. It was also where all the C-suite executives had their offices, each with their assistants sitting right outside their doors.

"I continue to be surprised with how things work over here," Adrian said. "It's a whole different world, and not at all what I expected, especially the politics. I'm just not cut from that cloth. Sometimes I wonder if I'll ever get used to it, and if I did the right thing uprooting my family so I could take this job."

Then Adrian seemed to catch himself. "Don't get me wrong, I wanted this role. I'm very appreciative of the opportunity and committed to making it work. This is a dream job, and I'd be a fool to think otherwise."

"Well," I responded, "sometimes the fool is he who *doesn't* think otherwise. I'm sure things will unfold as they need to."

I looked forward to helping Adrian adjust to his new environment. The question was what exactly would need adjusting for this role to work.

Adrian Uncovers His Hidden Blocker

At our first coaching meeting a few weeks later, I started by asking Adrian what had attracted him to the CSO position in the first place. His face lit up.

"I'm a strategy guy through and through," he said. "When I left consulting to go internal, I made sure I took on a role where the skills I came with would be highly valued and transferable. I've seen a lot of my consulting peers make the same transition, and they crash and burn. I wasn't about to do the same, and I really hit the jackpot here. Coming in and working with Jim, who I already had a relationship with through my consulting work, was so helpful. He gave me free rein to set up a strategy shop within the business he ran, and he trusted what I was doing. Now that I think about it, he acted as a buffer between my team and corporate so we wouldn't get distracted by whatever was happening at headquarters. That freed us up to be heads-down on the business and able to build a strong strategic discipline in our processes and way of thinking.

"So, when the opportunity came up to do that at scale across all the businesses, I jumped at it. Everything seemed to line up—the CEO had announced that developing new strategic priorities was top priority, I'd still get to work alongside Jim but now as his peer, and I was definitely intrigued by the track record of this position. Martin spent a few years in this role back in the day and look at him now—he's CEO. So I knew it was a lauded position and I couldn't turn it down."

"Now that you've been in it for a while, how do you feel?" I asked.

"Well, we're making great traction on the strategic priorities, but things aren't going like I hoped they would. Martin doesn't really engage with me in discussions I consider strategic; he still goes to my predecessor, Amanda. He'll raise some questions to the group at our SLT meetings, and then later, I'll hear that the questions were really aimed at me. Then there's the business presidents. With the exception of Jim, they just seem to oppose everything my team recommends. They complain that we're generating more work for them by meddling in what they're doing, and they've taken on a pretty adversarial stance with me. I'm not sure how to get through to them. There seem to be alliances on the tenth floor, and I'm not part of the inner circle."

Signs You May Have This Hidden Blocker

What you may see and feel

You feel alone, excluded, that you don't fit in.

You feel others don't bring you into discussions.

You feel like your work should speak for itself and anything else is politicking.

You often doubt yourself and worry about whether you have what it takes to be successful in your role.

You take cues from others on how you're doing based on how they engage with you. It's disconcerting when you don't know where you stand.

What others may see and feel

You need constant reassurance that you're valued and performing well.

You wait to be invited to participate rather than self-initiate.

You don't speak up at meetings unless asked to do so.

You'd rather stay heads-down in your work than engage in relationship-building.

You seem flustered or deferential in the face of pushback from your bosses or peers and don't assert your point of view.

Again, Adrian seemed to catch him himself. "It's probably not as bad as I'm making it out to be," he said. "They're all good people and we're all trying to do our best. But I do feel there's a real difference in how to make things happen in the C-suite, and I haven't figured out what that is. I just want to do what I was brought in to do—build an enterprisewide strategic discipline—but instead I feel like I'm spending most of my energy dealing with all the politicking that goes on in corporate. I don't like playing that game. It's not me. Actually, let me correct that. Not only do I not like playing that game, I don't even know what game we're playing."

"And how does that make you feel?"

"Like I'm not a true member of the team. Not being able to figure out the game makes me feel like I'll never fit in here and maybe shouldn't have gotten this job in the first place."

"Is that what you think? That you're not a member of the team?"

"Yeah, I guess so. Most of the time, I'm like, *What the heck am I doing here?* It's pretty sad, isn't it? I finally have a seat at the table. But it sure *doesn't feel like I belong* at the table or that the seat is mine."

Adrian Unpacks His Hidden Blocker

I could hear the uncertainty in Adrian's voice. I felt for him, as I've felt for the many leaders I've worked with who've struggled with the sense that they don't deserve their role or their place at their organization, no matter how much their accomplishments and expertise attest otherwise. Impostor syndrome, also known as the impostor phenomenon, can happen to leaders of any background, industry, years of experience, or level of seniority, and it's surprisingly common. Studies have found that up to 80 percent of people experience impostor feelings. It's especially pronounced among those from underrepresented groups such as women and younger workers, and people of color who experience "racialized impostor phenomenon," or the feelings of intellectual or professional self-doubt that arise due to experiences, systems, or principles of racial oppression and inequity.[1] Whatever the source, the impostor phenomenon is closely associated with reduced job performance, lower job satisfaction, and a higher risk of burnout.[2] This represents the experience of a *lot* of people who are feeling inadequate and unhappy at work, despite being high-achieving individuals with demonstrable successes.

I needed to hear more from Adrian about why he felt he didn't belong.

"Let's continue with the idea of you having a seat at the table," I said. "Can you think of what *would* need to happen to make it feel like the seat is actually yours?"

"For starters," he said, "Martin would come directly to me with questions. I mean he's the CEO and he has a right to speak to whomever he wants, but I do wonder why he doesn't reach out to me instead of Amanda. It would also help if the business leads were more collaborative rather than pushing back every step of the way and each doing their own thing. During our SLT meetings, there'd be room on the agenda to discuss strategy; instead, everyone is worried about the process we're going to use, and I never get to share our latest thinking on the strategy itself. To be honest, there's also this weird dynamic on the leadership team; it seems like a lot of conversations happen behind closed doors before and after meetings that I'm not privy to."

"What do you think that's about?"

"Well, on my better days, I think it's because that's just the way they do things. On my not-so-good days, I think it's because they don't want me in those conversations and perhaps I'm not the strategy head they were hoping for. Amanda was great in this role, and I was told I'd have big shoes to fill. I know I have the strategy chops to do this job, but sometimes I wonder if I have the other stuff it takes, especially the political savvy. So, on those days, I think I'm not included because they don't see me in the role. I mean, if they did, they'd invite me to those meetings, right?"

"I don't know. Maybe they would. Maybe they wouldn't. They're not the ones sitting in front of me right now to ask. So maybe it would help to hear what the rest of the leadership team thinks about you to help calibrate how they've experienced you as CSO so far. What do you think?"

"That makes me nervous, but sure, let's do it," Adrian said.

Over the following weeks, I met individually with Adrian's peers and the CEO and asked what they valued in Adrian to date and what suggestions they had for him as he continued to onboard into his new role.

In terms of strengths, the consensus seemed to be around Adrian's fresh perspectives, his ability to be collaborative, and the rich, deeply informed strategic background he brought. Several people highlighted how easy it was to partner with and get along with Adrian, and what a welcome addition he was to the SLT. "He's brought rigor, fresh thinking, and a willingness to challenge how functions have operated in the past," said one peer. "He's full of ideas and brought back the discipline of business strategy in a way we haven't had in a while." Another observed that Adrian was "improving and fine-tuning the company's strategic processes and raising our game overall in how we think about strategy."

As for what they'd like to see more of from Adrian, it was clear the leadership team wanted him to take more ownership of his role and be more proactive. "I would like to see him assert himself more," said one of his colleagues. "He's too deferential and has been slow to gain confidence. In a lot of our SLT discussions, he's more of a passive observer than an active participant . . . He seems apprehensive to voice his opinion, with our CEO especially. Instead of getting issues out on the table, he waits to see where the CEO is pointing and then follows."

Another colleague echoed the concern about Adrian's lack of confidence, even going so far as to say Adrian had "an inferiority complex," but she brought further nuance to the topic of the SLT meetings. "There's a culture here of 'the meeting before the meeting' to socialize things and bring people along before we present in front of Martin," she said. "Adrian hasn't really taken to that. He prefers impromptu discussions in the larger group, but the problem is, it puts people on the spot if they're not prebriefed. And because Adrian misses out on those early discussions, he ends up being tentative in the wider meetings. He tends to poll the room before offering an opinion of his own, and in this role, he should be the one driving the conversation about how the enterprise approaches strategy."

When I debriefed the feedback with Adrian, his initial reaction was to feel deflated.

"I guess I have a lot to work on," he said, "but I'm disappointed no one told me any of this. I've been CSO for over six months and I'm just hearing all this now. If they wanted me to push more in our meetings or have pre-meetings with them, they should have asked."

"Did you ask them what they wanted, or for their expectations?" I said. "Your initial reaction is questioning why your colleagues didn't ask for what they wanted from you, which is fair and certainly would have made things easier. But how about you? What did you do to make this transition easier or harder for yourself?"

"Well, I didn't feel like I needed to ask how they wanted me to deal with them. I'm a quick study, and I picked up pretty fast how they do things. Like I said, it just feels like a lot of politicking, and I don't operate that way."

"And as a result of that?"

"I kind of opted out."

"And what was the result for you?"

"I ended up feeling like I'm not part of the group—like I don't belong here."

"Yes. Listen, I'm not absolving others of their actions," I said. "They certainly played their part. But so have you. I have this vision of you really wanting to be invited to a party and then getting an invitation and actually going to the party, but then not wanting to be there. Here's the thing, Adrian—if you've been invited to the party and you're at the party, you belong. Now, whether you accept how others behave and they accept how you behave is a different story. But before we get there, let's just establish that by choosing to be on the senior leadership team—by accepting your invitation to be there—you belong. Period."

"I can see that," he said after pausing a bit. "I think I was waiting for others to make me feel like I have a seat at the table rather than just *acting* like it's mine. I guess a lot of the reason I feel like I don't fit in has probably been of my own doing."

"You're in a vicious cycle," I said. "You want others to include you to feel like you belong. Meanwhile, others want you to opt in more because you already do belong. You wait. They wait. It's a pattern. But the only thing that's in your control is to break *your* part of the pattern—the part that you own and that you have control over."

Adrian seemed to be taking it all in.

"What's landing with you, Adrian?"

"I've been so resistant to how the SLT does things that I've separated myself from the team before even getting started. So, in a way, I never gave them a chance. And I haven't really given myself a chance either. I didn't see belonging as a choice. I think what I'm getting out of this conversation is whether I think I belong or not is up to me. It's a choice I need to make."

While it's important that we don't absolve others of their actions, especially if they intentionally exclude a colleague, what Adrian was starting to realize was that just because others were different from him or went about things in a different way didn't mean he didn't *belong* to the group. In other words, uniformity isn't required to belong. That was just the story he was telling himself, which eventually led to even more disconnection from his peers—which in turn weakened his impact.

As an assignment, I asked Adrian to note all the times the thought "I don't belong here" ran through his mind over the course of the coming week. I told him to have a Post-it note for each day and to write a check mark every time he noticed that thought. At our next meeting, Adrian laid out all his Post-it notes. Some had dozens of check marks.

"Well, here you go," he said, laughing.

"I love it!" I responded. "OK, so what's your takeaway from this exercise?"

"First of all, I noticed that this thought comes up way more than I ever realized," he said. "That surprised me. And even more so, it didn't just happen in relation to the SLT. I noticed it in other aspects too. One example is when the CEO asked me to jump on a call with him and two board members. I felt really uncomfortable, almost nervous—and I remember thinking maybe he should have asked someone else, that I didn't belong on that call. Then another time was outside of work. I was out to dinner with my kids and my wife, and they were all laughing while my kids told stories about the latest teen drama going on with their friends. And I just felt like I was an outsider looking in—that it wouldn't even matter if I was there or not. That one really hit home for me because there was a time when I felt close to my kids, and I'd take them to their sports games and help them practice. But as they've become teenagers, I just don't feel that connection and like they even want me around. And the stuff they talk about quite frankly seems superfluous, so I don't engage much. So, yeah, not only do I feel on the outside looking in at work, it happens at home too. It's disconcerting to feel like I'm an outsider so often."

"I understand. Let me ask you this—I know it wasn't the assignment, but did you notice any moments when you felt like you *did* belong?"

He shared that he had—with his direct report team, and when he was out on the water with his crew team.

"With those groups," Adrian explained, "it just feels like they want me there. All those other examples, not so much."

"It's interesting to me how you went straight to what others do to make you feel like you do or don't belong," I said. "It makes me think there's this underlying assumption on your end that others are responsible for your sense of belonging. Is that true?"

"Well, shouldn't others make you feel welcome and included? Am I wrong in expecting that?"

"I'm not here to say whether you're wrong or right, Adrian. I'm just asking whether that expectation—that others are solely responsible to make you feel like you're a part of the group—serves you."

"True," said Adrian, "I guess I've always felt like whether or not I belong is contingent on how others act toward me rather than this steadfast belief that no matter what others do or think, I still belong. It's like I need validation."

"Validation of what? Because to be valid means to be accepted."

"I think what it comes down to is that I've looked to others for cues that I'm accepted. It's like I'm always wondering if what I'm bringing to the table is acceptable to everyone. Except sometimes I probably just assume from the get-go that it won't be, and I hold back. I guess I subconsciously tell myself that if I don't show up fully, it saves me from the possible outcome of not being accepted."

"You make a great point there," I said. "You can't be rejected from a role if you don't fully show up for it, can you?"

Adrian's "I don't belong here" hidden blocker was there because, like everyone's, it was serving a purpose. Most of the time, this blocker serves to protect us from the fear of rejection or of not measuring up. Telling ourselves that we don't fit in or won't be welcomed into a group can often give us justification for avoiding situations, thereby preempting the pain we'd feel if others don't include us, or diminishing the sting of rejection if we do try and don't get the results we're hoping for. When someone rejects your proposal, for example, that hidden blocker is there to say, "See, I told you you don't belong here, and if you had heeded my warning, you wouldn't feel disappointed and embarrassed!" So, in a way, it provides a softer landing because you were already expecting the disappointment.

"I can see how I've done this a lot in my professional *and* personal life," Adrian went on. "I've used what others signal as ways to determine if I fit in or not."

"Look, inherent in what you're saying is that in order to feel like you belong somewhere, you need to feel accepted. All I'm suggesting is that there may be a difference between the two. That to feel like you belong is one thing and to be accepted is another. What's the difference for you, if any?"

"I hadn't thought about it that way. To be accepted is passive and at the mercy of others," he said. "But to belong is up to me.

Potential Costs of This Hidden Blocker

Missed opportunities: Leaders may opt out of situations where they anticipate they won't fit in. In effect, they disqualify themselves before others can do so, thus avoiding the potential pain of rejection or not fitting in. Or, as they frequently downplay their accomplishments and doubt themselves, they may not try for promotions and other opportunities to advance and grow.

Weak organizational network: Fearful of being rejected, some leaders isolate themselves, neglecting the need to build key relationships. This keeps them out of the informal information flow and weakens their opportunity to influence.

Inauthenticity and lack of trust: Leaders who worry they don't belong may try to gauge their contributions according to what will appeal to the group. When they make a habit of saying what they think others want to hear rather than what they really think, they can come across as inauthentic, too political,

I'm already in the seat; I'm at the table. So why am I waiting for others to accept me to make me feel like I'm a legit member of the group? The sheer fact that I'm there means I'm part of the group—whether they accept me or not is a different question and one that I don't have full control over but can certainly try to influence."

"If that's the case, what is within your control that would make you feel like you belong?" I asked.

"Well, what I now realize is external validation is clearly out of my control and will never make me feel like I belong. What is in my control is just fundamentally knowing the value I bring to the table. And that's something that has to come from within. I know what that is with my direct report team and my crew team, but not so much with the SLT . . . or with my kids anymore. I've got to figure out what that is if I want to feel like I belong."

or manipulative, which threatens the sense of trust and psychological safety teams need to perform well.

Reluctance to take risks: A sense of not belonging, and certainly of outright rejection, can cause leaders to feel unsure of themselves, indecisive, or tentative. Without sufficient confidence and the assurance that their peers and teams have their back, they play it safe and hold back on their participation and decisions.

Adverse impact on well-being: In an effort to prove to themselves that they deserve to be there, these leaders often place very high standards on themselves, often succumbing to perfectionism and overwork, and at a higher risk for anxiety and depression.[a]

a. US Department of Health and Human Services, "Our Epidemic of Loneliness and Isolation, 2023: The U.S. Surgeon General's Advisory on the Healing Effects of Social Connection and Community," 2023, https://www.hhs.gov/sites/default/files/surgeon-general-social-connection-advisory.pdf.

The Roots of This Hidden Blocker

A sense of belonging is so critical to our well-being that in his famous "hierarchy of needs" pyramid, psychologist Abraham Maslow ranked "love and belonging" as the third most important need, only after basic physiological requirements such as food and water, and the need for safety and security. More recent research has shown that having close relationships with others is critical for healthy human development and well-being, so much so that many people prefer to be in the company of strangers rather than be alone.[3]

There are a number of reasons we can feel like we don't belong. Sometimes it's a temporary feeling prompted by circumstances that place us in unfamiliar territory. Other times it's more of a persistent mindset that stays with us no matter the circumstances. In Adrian's case, the promotion seemed to spark acute feelings of being "an outsider looking in," but the more he reflected on his experience, the more he realized this unconscious belief had been driving his behavior and his feelings of not belonging in different areas of his life for many years. The promotion had simply intensified those feelings, rendering them no longer undeniable.

Some common experiences that can lead to this blocker include:

- *Moving to a new company or starting a new role.* This can easily disrupt one's sense of belonging until new connections are made and proficiency is established.

- *Not fitting organizational norms.* This is a broad category that can include anything from being a member of an underrepresented group to feeling that you're not a good fit with the company culture to having values that are different from the majority's, and more. Anything that causes you to feel different from the dominant group can contribute to a sense of not belonging.

- *Being in a highly competitive environment.* Research psychologist Kevin Cokley has noted that highly stressful and competitive environments can be incubators for impostor feelings, which leads one to feel they don't deserve to be where they are and don't belong.[4]

- *Being rejected in the past.* Neuroscience shows that the pain of being socially rejected activates the same neural pathways as those involved in physical pain, and the effect is so potent that even an indirect experience of rejection (that is, watching a video of disapproving faces) triggers the same response.[5] The sting of these experiences can linger for many years.

- *Needing external validation.* Relying solely on others' approval or affirmation for our sense of belonging means we're at risk for feeling unworthy anytime that external validation isn't forthcoming. Further, experiencing negative feedback or failure can spark feelings of shame, leading us to feel we don't fit in because we're flawed in some way, or don't measure up to others' standards.

At times, more so than I wish were the case, the feeling of not belonging is not of our own doing but due to the fact that others are indeed intentionally excluding us. This is especially challenging when the exclusion is systemic, such as when sexism, racism, ableism, or some other form of bias comes into play and affects a person or group of people. Leaders who are one of the "only, first, or few" at work—for example, the only Black executive, the first manager with a disability, one of the few women in leadership—are often treated like they don't belong, no matter how qualified they are for the role. Within systems of exclusion, leaders can easily internalize the belief that they don't belong, circumscribing their vision of what is achievable. Meanwhile, this limiting belief is one that is continuously perpetuated by the very system that created it in order to maintain the status quo. Such a system often causes and exacerbates impostor syndrome in excluded groups, and rightfully, there is a very strong argument that if we want individuals to not experience impostor syndrome, the system itself needs to change.[6] The question is what can one do in the meantime? At the end of the day, whether the cause of this hidden blocker is due to circumstantial context or systemic bias, you are faced with the question of whether or not it serves you to hold on to that belief. And for most leaders I work with, the answer is no.

In Adrian's case, he recognized how his need for external validation was keeping him from fully taking his seat at the table and reinforcing his blocker that he didn't belong in the C-suite. Many of us learn early on to rely on the surrounding group's approval for our sense of intrinsic worth, which is certainly easy to do, as well-meaning caregivers and teachers praise us for our accomplishments, and we learn to perform in order to secure the approval we need to feel OK and that we belong. Later, that dynamic easily translates into the workplace, where many leaders are highly motivated to pursue wins and achievements.

Now, as we all know, wins and achievements at work are encouraged and rewarded, and strong performance is necessary. And I want to be clear that there is nothing wrong with external validation per se; positive feedback is motivating and lets us know we're on the right track, and we all need to know our contributions are valued.

Problems arise, however, when leaders base their entire self-worth or sense of belonging on the worth or the acceptance they perceive others to have of them. When we rely *solely* on external validation, just as we saw with Adrian, the way others react to us (that is, if they include us or not, invite us or not, agree or disagree with us, praise or criticize us, and so on) becomes the primary indicator for how worthy we believe we are and if we feel we belong. And guess what? It's never enough, because circumstances and others' feelings are forever changing. Moreover, if we struggle with impostor feelings, external assurances are rarely persuasive.

That's why our sense of worth and belonging ultimately needs to be rooted in something deep and unwavering. According to renowned psychologist Robert Kegan, in the earlier stages of adult development, we look for external validation to derive our sense of who we are. But as we grow and mature, we gain an independent identity, one that is not built on others' opinions or the fear of disapproval. In the near-final stage of adult development, which only 35 percent of the adult population reaches, according to Kegan, we can define who we are and rely on our own internal sense of direction, rather than be defined and guided by other people, our relationships, or our environment.[7]

While we're still on the journey to that stage, we can learn to locate our sense of belonging in more steadfast sources—an inner conviction, a shared commitment, a sense of mission or purpose, a trusted group. When my twins were starting elementary school, we decided to send them to a private school that, while diverse, was predominantly white. We knew that unless we proactively continued to cultivate it, the sense of belonging they'd built thus far as Black children could be torn down pretty quickly, especially as they began to spend more time away from the family unit, and the external validation from peers became increasingly important. To prevent this hidden blocker from settling in and taking over, their dad and I made a conscious effort to ensure that their first sense of belonging was to themselves, and that we as a family would be their consistent home base no matter what. One of the most effective tools we used (and I must give their dad much of the credit) was a mantra we repeated over and over to them, beginning when they were five and that we still use as they launch into their young professional lives: "Don't get it twisted. It's not you who's lucky to be there. It's they who are lucky to have you. You belong wherever you are."

Adrian Unblocks from His Hidden Blocker

At our next meeting, I asked Adrian to imagine he was walking out of his next SLT meeting feeling like he belonged. "What would be different from the meetings you had, say, last week?" I asked.

"I would be speaking up a lot more, and I'd be more confident about where everyone stands on the discussion topics. I'm often surprised by others' reactions, but in this meeting, I'd be more in sync with everyone. I would know why I'm there; I'd know exactly what my role is in that meeting and that it's worthwhile. That's a big one for me. Until now, I don't think I quite grasped what my role was and was unknowingly waiting for someone to give me a sign or tell me."

"What I love about how you're framing this, Adrian, is that you're defining belonging and what having a seat at the table means for you, and these are all things under your control. That gives you way more agency than if you leave it to the whim of others. So how can you make all those things happen?"

"Fundamentally, I need to let go of this 'I don't belong here' thought that's playing in the background all the time. I have to start hanging on to the notion that 'I am here; therefore I belong.' That will open me up more to fulfilling my role rather than holding me back. I mean, at the end of the day, if I don't believe I belong with the SLT, why should they?"

"That's right. For your next meeting, I want you to prepare as though you have nothing to prove and you deserve to be there. What would a person who has zero doubts about their seat at the table do to prep for an SLT meeting? How would they act in the meeting? Even if it feels a little weird, I want you to think about it from that person's point of view and then make a list of the actions that person would take and *do them yourself.*"

When I next saw Adrian and asked him to debrief, I could see he was eager to share the results.

"That felt so different!" he exclaimed. "That was literally the best meeting I've had with the SLT. It's not that I didn't get any pushback or like all of a sudden the CEO was hanging on to every word I said. I just felt different and way better than I have in previous meetings."

"What did you do differently?"

"Well, it's like we discussed," he said. "I kept thinking, 'I already belong. There's nothing to prove.' Then I asked myself, If that's the case, what's the best way to prep for and act in this meeting? And I came up with three things. One, you're going to laugh, but I had some pre-meetings with each of the business heads. I know I've been kicking and screaming about not wanting to do that, but you know what? It helped tremendously, and it wasn't the waste of time I thought it would be, nor were they underhanded and back-channeling. I realize that given the competing agendas and the underlying tension the business heads face between meeting their P&L results and having to operate under the enterprise umbrella, these warm-up conversations help gain alignment and consensus ahead of the larger meeting. They're actually helpful, and if I'm going to have any chance of moving the needle with leadership, I've got to meet them where they are.

"The second big thing is I had a conversation with the CEO to learn more about what was on his mind as it relates to the strategic priorities. It helped me understand the tension he has with the board and how I can be more helpful to him in navigating his interactions with them. I also spoke to Amanda about what she found most effective in dealing with the CEO when she was in my role, and her advice was invaluable. I was able to go into the SLT and respond to the CEO's questions in a way that got a direct response from him rather than him having to circle back with her.

"Last, I had real clarity about what my role is in that meeting. When I looked at things from the perspective that I already belong, I immediately knew what I wanted to accomplish and how I wanted to come across. That really, really helped. I realize that when I'm with my direct report team, I don't have to think about it because it's just assumed; it doesn't even occur to me to wonder if I belong. And all this time, I've been waiting for it to happen on the SLT. I needed to be more proactive in putting a stake in the ground rather than waiting for everything to fall into place to make me feel worthy of being there. And you know what? I tried it out on my kids, too. I'm still not a fan of high school gossip, but it is important to me that I feel connected to my kids. So, I listened and asked them questions and also shared some of what's going on in my world. They were actually amused by some of the shenanigans I have to deal with at work."

"Adrian, look at you!" I said. "That's a lot of traction in a short amount of time. I'd love to hear what you're committing to do to help you sustain this feeling that you *do* belong."

Adrian took a few moments to jot down his thoughts in his notebook. When he was done, he slid it over to me so I could see what he wrote:

1. Be clear about my value proposition to the SLT and the company as CSO. What is the impact I make? What is the difference I make? Take stock every day of how I'm adding value.

2. Find the sweet spot where my agenda and my peers' agendas intersect and make that my starting point with them rather than just my side. Build relationships with them. Seek to understand them. Frame things in a way that is relevant to them.

3. Be proactive with the CEO. Don't wait to be asked. Figure out his pain points and help relieve them.

"I think I can do these things and not feel like I'm 'playing a game' as long as I realize they're actually part of my role," Adrian said. "I'm not faking it. I'm doing the job. I'm giving myself permission to fully step into the role. That will make a big difference in how I navigate this new world."

A key turning point for Adrian was realizing that he had always belonged, and that he, not others, was the one standing in the way of his ability to believe it and lead from that place. Once he was able to accept that, he could see how to lead with authenticity in a way that was aligned with his values while still honoring the differences in the rest of the SLT and the way things were done on the tenth floor. Finally able to lead from a starting point of belonging, Adrian was free to interact with his new peers as an equal and make the impact he really wanted to.

Coach Yourself

Have you ever struggled with the sense that you don't fit in at work, don't belong among your peers or colleagues, or don't deserve to be where you are? If you think your primary hidden blocker is "I don't belong here," first establish how this limiting belief shows up for you by naming it. Respond with reframed beliefs that can help you recognize and believe that you truly *do* belong, followed by action items that will help reinforce your new belief and make the impact you want.

From Blocked

- I don't belong here.

- I'm not good enough for this place (or role).

- I'm the wrong choice for this role.

- I don't fit in here.

- I don't make a difference here.

- I am an outsider.

- I feel like a fraud.

To Unblocked

- I belong wherever I am.

- I have every right to be here as much as everyone else.

- It's OK to feel different while still being part of the group.

- I am exactly where I need to be.

- My differences and unique perspectives are assets.

- It can take time to feel connected to the larger whole.

- My skills and expertise got me here; therefore, I belong.

To Action

- *Define your value proposition.* Clarify for yourself why you are the one in the role, the meeting, and so on. Be clear about the difference and impact you make.

- *Contribute your unique skills and insights.* Recognize the value you bring to the group by sharing your perspectives and expertise.

- *Remind yourself of shared goals or values with the group.* Focus on what unites you with others to strengthen your sense of belonging. Find the intersection between what's important to you and your stakeholders; let that lead your interactions.

- *Identify a few supportive people and build relationships with them.* Focus on cultivating meaningful connections rather than fitting in with everyone at once.

Part Three

Unblocked

Chapter 10

Helping Others Overcome Their Hidden Blockers

Each one, teach one.

—AFRICAN PROVERB

You've now worked through understanding how beliefs can influence your behavior, and how they have the potential to block you from achieving the results you want. You also know how to recognize when a hidden blocker is holding you back, and how to reframe that belief to one that inspires and supports your full potential as a leader. In short, you know how to move from blocked to unblocked.

With this knowledge in place, you're in a unique position to spark and support this same kind of development in others, using the same process you used to coach yourself. Once you've become aware of and successfully overcome your own hidden blockers, you can more easily spot them in others, even when their hidden blockers are different from your own, and you can play a vital role in helping those you supervise, manage, or mentor unblock from the beliefs that hold them back. Now that you know that stalled progress isn't always due to a tactical or skills issue and, instead, often stems from something deeper, you are able to pay it forward and help team members address their blockers at the source: on the inner stage where beliefs are formed.

This can happen passively, simply by role-modeling and leading from an unblocked state, which will naturally be reflected in your attitude, words, and actions. Indeed, research has shown that leadership carries a contagion effect, with leaders influencing the organization to such a degree that many of their behaviors—everything from technical and strategic skills to integrity and cooperation to the development of self and others—have been observed in their direct reports. Not surprisingly, high-performing and highly engaged leaders are much more likely to develop high-performing and highly engaged employees, and the effect can proliferate throughout the entire organization.[1]

Or it can happen more actively, when you are consciously engaged in helping to develop unblocked leadership in others. This kind of engagement calls for you to put on your coaching hat. If you really want to help develop your team to their fullest potential, you need to coach them to a different mindset, one that's built on the awareness of the role that beliefs play. You don't need any special expertise to help your team members free themselves of their hidden blockers. You need only use the same Blocked to Unblocked Roadmap you've already learned to use on yourself to usher them on the right path.

Note that this is all about *helping* and *guiding*—your job is not to solve problems or provide answers. Good coaches function as guides and facilitators, and as sources of motivation and accountability. You can be an essential partner in helping a colleague or team member realize they're blocked and then support them as they work through the roadmap, but ultimately, unblocking from hidden blockers will always be up to the individual.

Thus, this chapter isn't about teaching coaching skills; there are plenty of books on that. Instead, it will provide a glimpse into how you can harness the power of beliefs to improve performance, create change, and drive innovation in others such as your team members or direct reports, and then beyond to the broader organization.

Let's say a manager sees an employee struggling to participate in meetings. He gives the employee feedback and encouragement, and throws in a few tips on how to speak up—likely ones that worked for the manager himself. But this approach doesn't address the root cause of why the employee isn't contributing. And if the root cause is not addressed, the situation is sure to repeat itself. On the other hand, if the manager has successfully worked through his own hidden blockers, he can more easily spot them in his employee and can use a similar approach to help that person become unblocked—a true solution rather than a temporary or partial fix.

Unblocked Leadership in Action

Let's take a look at an example from one of my coaching clients who first did the work to become unblocked and then helped one of her team members break through the belief that was limiting his potential. Kelly was a principal at a consulting firm. She had engaged in coaching because she felt she was plateauing in her development and wanted to work with an objective observer who could point out any blind spots and help her see the bigger picture. One of her light-bulb moments occurred when she received feedback from her colleagues. While the feedback did not identify any glaring performance issues, Kelly realized there were discrepancies between how she thought she was coming across and how others were perceiving her. For example, she was fairly indirect when offering constructive criticism to her team, an approach she took out of politeness and a desire not to discourage. But several people interpreted it as Kelly being insufficiently invested in their development, and a few found her aloof.

Seeing the difference between her intent and her actual impact opened Kelly's eyes to how assumptions and impressions don't always square with on-the-ground reality. This led her to examine her beliefs to locate the point of breakdown between how she wanted to lead and how she was actually being experienced by those she was leading.

Not long after, Kelly found herself in a challenging situation with her mentee Tom, who had joined the firm ten months prior. Tom was an experienced professional with a wealth of knowledge from having spent years at another consulting firm. But his transition to manager hadn't gone smoothly. Kelly had held a few one-on-ones with him to share her observations and offer ideas for course correction, and while Tom had responded well, he always seemed to revert to his former patterns, his improvement fading after a few weeks. Now, Kelly was receiving troubling feedback not just from colleagues but from Tom's clients as well. It was clearly time for a different approach.

With her new understanding of how performance is impacted by beliefs, Kelly set out to coach Tom in a way that brought attention to his mindset and beliefs, rather than just the tactical-skills approach they'd tried in the past. Here's how she did it.

The first step was to help Tom realize he was blocked. Kelly did this by having him look at the impact of his behaviors and then following up with candid feedback on his most recent performance.

> *Kelly:* Tom, how do you think you're experienced by others right now—your team as well as your clients?

> *Tom:* Well, I think I drive my team to action, which is what's important. As for the clients, I'm eager to learn about their business so I can help them. I ask plenty of questions, so I think they see me as curious and wanting to help.

> *Kelly:* OK, let's break that down a little further. We'll start with your team. How do you think they experience you as a leader?

> *Tom:* I'm not exactly sure. It's not something I give much consideration to. If I had to guess, I'd say they experience me as driven, focused, and motivating. High-energy! I like things done yesterday.

> *Kelly:* And you said clients see you as curious and eager to help.

Tom: Definitely. I am those things, so I assume that comes across.

Kelly: I think some of your impressions are accurate—you're definitely driven and you do get your team to deliver. But based on what I'm seeing and the feedback I'm getting from others, I don't think your intentions always come through in your impact. May I give you some feedback?

Tom: Of course.

Kelly: The areas of concern boil down to two main points. In meetings with the partners, you take up a lot of airtime, even when it's not your meeting. I've seen that happening with your own team, too; you talk more than you listen, and you tend to issue directives rather than ask for their ideas.

Then with clients, it's a bit similar. They appreciate your enthusiasm and commitment, but they say you tend to tell them what to do rather than gain their buy-in to solutions. So, the bottom-line impact is that both colleagues and clients perceive you as being too heavy-handed, and rather than someone they call in as a trusted adviser, I'm afraid your pushing is alienating them.

Tom: Wow. I had a sense that some of my client relations were off, but I didn't realize people felt so strongly about my leadership style.

Kelly: The important thing is, now you do. It's helpful to have awareness before moving to action.

By giving the other person succinct, observable feedback that helps them see the impact they're having—not the one they *think* they're having or that they'd *like* to have—they start realizing they're blocked. Any time there is a gap between intent and impact, or a difference between the impact someone is actually having and what they need to have to be successful in the role, it's a good sign they're blocked. Unblocked leaders who operate in a coaching capacity are in an excellent position to help others come to their own realization of where that might be happening.

When it comes to the next step, helping others name their hidden blocker, this is where many people try to bypass the process. They either want to hurry things up and name it for their team member or avoid this step altogether and jump straight to tactics.

Why? As for the former, it *seems* as if naming another's hidden blocker will save everyone time and energy, and get your team member where they need to be more quickly. But I can tell you from experience that unless the person arrives at these conclusions themselves and internalizes them, any insights you give them aren't likely to last. Tom is an excellent example; he always improved temporarily after his meetings with Kelly, only to go right back to the patterns he was used to. This is what we all do, until we name and accept what's causing the problem.

As for why managers avoid working through this step with others, it's usually because they're uncomfortable with going beyond the surface. Frankly, it's simpler to operate on a tactical level, where you're dealing with discrete, observable skills that can be assessed by standard metrics. Dealing with internal matters of belief, especially when it comes to long-entrenched patterns that are so ingrained we don't realize they're there, much less constantly influencing our actions, is far more challenging. It's messier, because people are complex, and their histories are complicated. There are no guideposts etched in stone, no standardized way forward. It can be scary.

Let me offer a suggestion that will make your job easier: approach this step with curiosity. Curiosity is disarming—it helps to lessen people's defensive reactions. It also conveys your genuine interest in hearing what the other person has to say, and a willingness to explore their input together. Research has found that leaders who display curiosity make employees feel more psychologically safe, encourage them to speak up more, and get more results.[2] Contrast that approach with supplying answers, which shuts down dialogue and further self-examination, or being accusatory ("Let me tell you where you went wrong"), which erodes trust and others' willingness to explore their hidden blocker.

This really can be as easy as stating that you're curious. Here's how Kelly approached this step with Tom.

> *Kelly:* I'm curious. What do you think it is that leads you to tell people what they need to do?

> *Tom:* It's what I said earlier. I'm on the line to get results for clients, and I've got to hold my team's feet to the fire to get them. I don't want to waste any time. I just need to get it done.

It doesn't always happen as simply and cleanly as this, but be curious enough and you will eventually get there. Here are other questions you can ask to explore the possible limiting beliefs that are getting in your colleague's or team member's way:

- What were you thinking in the moment that made you approach the situation as you did (or make that decision)?

- What do you believe to be true about this situation?

- When you think back to the situation, what is the underlying assumption you held about yourself? About the other people involved? The situation itself?

- What's the mindset that's getting in your way of achieving the results you want?

Once named, your job is then not to refute or debate their belief. Your role is simply to help bring it to light, and you do so by helping them identify it and then acknowledging it. Only then can you move to questioning whether that belief is serving them vis-à-vis their goal.

As we've seen in the previous chapters, it's natural for any of us to defend our hidden blockers. When defensiveness arises, realize that you have an opportunity to help the person loosen their grip on their limiting belief so they can explore other mindsets that would be more helpful. The key is to refrain from being judgmental or admonishing them. Now is not the time to say, "No. You're wrong. You shouldn't think that way" or even to point out there's a better way. Rather, acknowledge what they think and feel, and offer questions that help them start seeing past the defensive wall. Remember that acknowledgment does not mean agreement, so don't let your own defensiveness or impatience get in the way of helping your colleague get unblocked.

When Tom's defenses went up—which is exactly what happened as the meeting with Kelly continued—Kelly made sure to stay in coaching mode to help him work through it as well as to bring it back to him and his beliefs and behaviors.

> *Tom:* I really don't see anything wrong with wanting to get things done efficiently. And I also think this feedback is confusing. Weren't we all told that client results are a priority?

> *Kelly:* I see how the feedback comes across that way, and I understand your frustration. I don't want this to be the case moving forward. We do have a lot of external feedback to consider, though, and the majority of it is about how you're interacting with colleagues and clients in a way that negatively impacts results. I'm wondering what part you see you've played in creating the dynamic you're now facing with others?

> *Tom:* If I had to zero in on something, it again goes back to the thought that I really *have* to get things done, which I guess makes me over-rotate when it comes to how I'm treating people. I can see how I can come across as pushy.

Here are other questions you can ask your colleague to help them move past their defensiveness:

- What part of this situation do you own?

- What's in your control?

- How is what you're thinking aligned with your end goal?

Deconstructing the hidden blocker is another part of the process that many want to bypass due to their own limiting beliefs about—dare I say it—intimacy at work. And by that I'm referring to the cliché definition of intimacy as "in-to-me-see," or letting people see past your exterior persona, which requires vulnerability. Here are common ways leaders will try to dismiss or sidestep this crucial part of the process with others:

- I don't want to get into their personal business.

- They won't want to share on that level.

- This is too personal for the workplace.

- This is just too "woo-woo."

- They should be talking to a therapist or executive coach about this kind of stuff, not me.

But here's the deal: if you really want to help develop your team members to their fullest potential, you will have to bring coaching into your suite of leadership skills. Your role is not to be a therapist (nor should you be), and you are not required to become a certified executive coach. But you do need to be able to coach your teams effectively, and any effective coaching discussion depends on your ability to see at least some of what's going on inside of them, not just the outside.

Because all those actions that are helping or hindering your team member's performance? They are driven by interior beliefs. And there are endless external forces that help forge, sustain, and amplify these beliefs. It's an endless give-and-take that affects all of us, so there's no way around it. If you want to coach someone in a way that's sustainable—that doesn't just address symptoms, if you will, but root causes—you have to at least help them acknowledge and see what's happening internally.

To that end, encourage the person you're coaching to deconstruct their own hidden blocker; don't deconstruct it yourself. A simple invitation often suffices.

Kelly: This "I just need to get it done" belief—where is that coming from for you?

Now, Kelly goes into active listening mode and lets Tom speak extemporaneously. If he gets stuck, she can offer a short, supportive question, but for the most part, she remains quiet while he answers or finds his way to an answer by thinking aloud. Remaining (mostly) silent prevents you from trying to explain what's happening or to share your own opinions and theories as to where the other person's beliefs may have originated. The intention here is to create the space where your colleague can start thinking about the origin of their belief without you pushing, forcing, or projecting anything onto them.

And if their response is "I don't know" or they flat out refuse to go further, don't push. Just share a story of one of your own limiting beliefs and its origin. Or offer an invitation to explore at a later time, such as "I've often found it helpful to reflect on why I think the way I do and if those beliefs are helping me reach my goals, so perhaps you might want to try that when you're ready," and let it rest. You planted the seed; now let your colleague water it and cultivate it as they need to.

Here are other questions you can ask to encourage someone to deconstruct their hidden blocker:

- What shaped this belief?

- What reinforced this belief?

- How has this belief helped you?

- Where did you learn to think in that way?

- How did that become your default belief?

Once your colleague sees and understands the role their mindset and their thoughts are playing in keeping them from their goal, then you can move on to unblocking from the hidden blocker that's currently holding them back. This is where you will help them reframe their belief or shape a new mindset that's aligned with the impact they want to have.

In Tom's case, driving for client results was his primary goal. But his belief of "I just need to get it done" was getting in the way of earning the buy-in and building the relationships to get to the results he desired. It wasn't the impact that needed to change but his way of thinking, which would lead to a different approach that would help him create that impact. Again, Kelly's role was not to tell Tom how to think but rather to help him discover that for himself.

> *Kelly:* What do you need to believe about your approach to move you closer to getting results with our clients?
>
> *Tom:* I have to believe that getting buy-in is as important, if not more important, than getting to a solution quickly. I also have to expand my mindset that building relationships, listening, and getting buy-in *is* part of "getting it done." The bottom line is I need to shift from "I just need to get it done" to "We want to get it done."

Asking questions that help others entertain alternative ways of thinking allows them to start seeing how a new mindset may break the pattern they're in. Here are other questions you can ask your colleague to help them reframe their beliefs:

- What mindset would be more helpful to you in this situation?

- How else can you think about yourself (or the other people involved) that would help move things forward?

- What do you need to believe to move you closer to your goal?

- How would you need to think differently about this to get the results you want?

With a reframed belief in hand, you can then help your colleague move to action, to determine what behaviors would be more aligned with their new mindset. Simply asking what they can do that will fall in line with their new belief can yield a list of action items. When Kelly asked Tom this very question, they went on to create a quick list of actions that reinforced his desired shift from "I just need to get it done" to "We want to get it done," which included reminders he could carry into every interaction:

- Listen more than speak in meetings.

- Ask for others' input and *suggest* solutions rather than tell others what to do.

- Check for alignment rather than assume it's the case.

- Pull rather than push.

By articulating actions that are aligned with the more supportive belief, they can keep themselves honest. If they're not getting the impact they want, it's likely that the belief and actions are not aligned. In Tom's case, every time he defaulted back to his heavy-handed behaviors, he was quick to check his mindset, and he'd realize he was back in "I just need to get it done" mode. By reframing, he could course-correct his actions to bring him closer to becoming the trusted adviser he wanted to be—and that others needed him to be.

. . .

Not all coaching conversations have the ending we want or expect, because sometimes it's not about moving the person forward to what you want or even what they want. Many times, it's about just helping them understand what's going on that's causing the challenge or tension they're experiencing so that they can determine their next step.

For example, I once had a client who was spearheading tremendous change in her organization. While most of her senior team was buying into her vision and the new priorities and initiatives she was putting in place, there was one leader who seemed resistant. Deliverables didn't meet expectations. Deadlines were missed. He'd agree to one thing in a meeting and do another. After months of providing feedback, setting expectations, and spending time with this leader to gain buy-in, my client was still seeing no movement and even more resistance from him, and was at her wits' end. During a coaching session where we worked on her own mindset, she started wondering what beliefs her colleague had about the changes taking place at the organization.

At their next weekly one-on-one, she asked him, "What do you believe about your role relative to where we're headed as an organization?"

He thought about it for a moment and then responded, "I think the value I bring as a leader and how I want to contribute and what you and the organization need from my role moving forward are not at all aligned."

Bringing this belief out in the open allowed them to candidly discuss the heart of the matter, which gave them the first chance at a truly productive discussion. Ultimately, the team member moved to a different role. It wasn't the outcome either of them had expected or necessarily would've chosen. But it allowed my client to move forward with what she wanted to accomplish and the team member to operate in a way and in a place more aligned with his interests.

Helping the Organization Unblock

Helping others unblock from their limiting beliefs isn't just important at an individual level. Leading at scale means being able to lead yourself, your team, and possibly even your organization. Even if you're not in the C-suite, through the contagion effect, your leadership influence always extends past your own team or division. And it's worth remembering that every person in an organization, no matter where they are in the hierarchy, has an effect on others, because they're all part of an interconnected and interdependent system. Individual development and organizational development are never mutually exclusive: as each person frees themselves of their hidden blockers and begins to perform at a higher level, they, in turn, uplevel the organization.

Of course, the higher up the chain you are, the wider your sphere of influence. And if it becomes apparent that changes need to be made on an organizational level—things like changing the culture, building bench strength, improving morale, driving growth, and creating more equity at scale—it requires an examination of the *collective* beliefs of leadership. As Albert Einstein aptly said, "The significant problems we face cannot be solved at the same level of thinking we were at when we created them." That's true of organizations too, which can be slow to change because of their sheer size and complexity. But often, it's because capital-L Leadership— whatever body is setting strategy and making decisions that affect the entire system—is in the grips of one or more hidden blockers writ large, and they, like individuals, are trying to remediate their "significant problems" with external tactics, rather than giving heed to the collective beliefs that gave rise to them. "The organizational system," observes leadership expert Bob Anderson, "cannot organize at a higher stage of development than the consciousness of the leadership."[3]

At a collective level, limiting beliefs can sound like:

- "This is the way it's always been done."

- "Failure is not an option."

- "Stay in your lane."

- "That's not our job."

- "This way has always served us well."

- "We need to remain loyal to our original vision."

Often, corporate hidden blockers are the unwritten rules and unspoken assumptions of leadership, and they trickle down throughout the organization. So once again, we must back up and start with the beliefs that are driving the behavior.

Nowhere is this truer in the workplace than when trying to drive strategic systems and culture change in an organization. Everyone may agree that the culture, structures, and policies need to change. But what also needs to change is the collective *mindset* of leadership that created and upheld the culture, structures, and policies that are no longer working. The bottom line is that it's not enough to *say* you want more innovation at the company, or that you need to break out of your silos, or that you value diversity and inclusion, or that you want to create a culture that fosters collaboration. You must actually *build the conditions* that will allow for the values and objectives you're going for.

And to accomplish that, you must first get your mind right. How does leadership as a group need to think differently to be able to enact those claims and intentions? What does the collective mindset need to be?

Many organizations remain stuck because leadership says they want one thing, but their thinking is not aligned with that desired outcome. For example, the leadership team that says that work-life balance is critical and wants to decrease the sense of burnout employees are reporting, but also believe that being always available is a sign of competence and drive. What happens when leadership holds this belief? Employees who are "always on" are rewarded, and thus the behavior is reinforced, and the disconnect between the organization's intentions and their impact continues.

Other examples: the leadership team that wants to increase representation of people of color in the organization but then believes it can't find qualified candidates. Or the leadership team that wants to encourage innovation among the ranks but then believes that failure is not an option, which discourages people from taking risks. When leadership's collective mindset is not aligned with the organizational culture desired, it's virtually impossible to create a new culture and to get the rest of the organization to shift their thinking (and thus their behavior). "There is no organizational transformation without a preceding transformation in the consciousness of the leadership," Anderson observes, and he's absolutely right.[4]

How do we achieve a transformation in corporate consciousness that sparks a transformation in organizational culture?

It starts with individual leaders becoming aware and doing the inner mindset work to become free of their own hidden blockers. Unblocked leaders are better positioned to shed light on any corporate hidden blockers that are keeping their organization stagnant. They are better equipped to raise the collective mindset of the organization, liberating it from the limiting beliefs that are keeping every part of the system, from individual contributors to the organization as a whole, from reaching their full potential. One by one by one, unblocked leaders can join forces to change entire systems and cultures.

This is the gift and the power and the calling of unblocked leadership.

The Road Ahead

Nothing will work unless you do.

—MAYA ANGELOU

We've reached the end of our journey together. Now what? While I'd love to say that you've arrived at your destination and your work is done, that is not the case.

If there's one thing I hope you take away from this book, it's that you can't always control what happens on the outside—a nasty email from a colleague, an urgent request from your boss, a promotion decision that didn't go your way, a downturn in the market—but you *can* control how you respond. And that makes all the difference in how you lead.

There is a Buddhist teaching called the parable of the second arrow that goes as follows:

> *The Buddha once asked his student, "If a person is struck by an arrow, is it painful?" The student nodded, yes. The Buddha then asked, "If a person is struck by a second arrow, is that even more painful?" The student again nodded, yes.*

The Buddha explained, "The first arrow in life we cannot control, but the second arrow is our reaction to the first. The second arrow is optional."

Difficulty is unavoidable in leadership. We cannot control every situation or person that crosses our path. We cannot avoid the changes, the challenges, and the conflicts, no matter how hard we try. This is the first arrow, and when it hits, it's painful.

But we can control the second arrow, which is the cause of much of our suffering at work and elsewhere. We can control the reaction we have to the pain of the first arrow, which will either compound our suffering or diminish its impact. If we react by repeating the patterns of our hidden blockers, we direct the second arrow straight into the tender spot of familiar territory: frustration, anger, resentment, stalled growth, burnout.

But if we take a moment, check our mindset about what's happening, and choose how to think and respond in this situation, the second arrow loses its power.

Moving from blocked to unblocked is not about avoiding the first arrow—any of the challenges that will always occur in the day-in and day-out of leadership. It's about moving through them with more ease because you are not hit by the second arrow of suffering caused by your limiting beliefs.

This work, the inner work of breaking free from our hidden blockers, never ends. Just when you think you've moved past, let go of, or overcome the belief that was getting in your way, it shows up again, and often it's the same old thought in more sophisticated garb. So, the goal is not to banish your hidden blockers or somehow eliminate them for good. Counterintuitively, it's to draw closer to them and be with them—befriend them, even—so you can understand why they're there and what needs they are fulfilling. This is how they begin to loosen their grip and how you prevent them from leading you. It takes practice, and it takes courage, to go through the unblocking process repeatedly and habitually. While you are in that practice, let me give you a few travel tips for the road ahead:

Give yourself grace. Here's the thing, you *will* backslide from time to time. The path from blocked to unblocked is not smooth and linear. Just as it does no good for me to become frustrated, annoyed, or blameful when my clients default to limiting beliefs and ineffective behaviors, it does you no good to react in those ways when you're coaching yourself. Instead, meet yourself exactly where you are—no blame, no shame—and use the tools offered in these pages to support yourself as you move forward. You are doing the best you can at every moment.

Don't go it alone. While my goal in writing this book is to help you coach yourself, that doesn't mean you always have to do this work alone. Leading can already feel lonely as it is. It's OK, even encouraged, to ask others for support, motivation, and accountability. Hiring a coach to support you through your unblocked journey is certainly an option. But it's not the only one. Work through the book with a friend, mentor, or colleague, and peer-coach each other. Make uncovering your hidden blockers a team effort as you examine your individual and collective beliefs together. Come back to the stories in these pages that most resonate with you for guidance and take comfort in knowing you are not alone.

Practice patience. If you're like me, you want results and you want them fast. I've learned the hard way that doing the inner work will always be a work in progress, and rushing through it will not make it any more effective. There is no timeline, no due dates, and no big, loud milestone announcement when you've unblocked from a hidden blocker. Instead, it's a slow, subtle unfolding where learnings are revealed to you in their own time and often quietly when you least expect it. Many times, you won't even realize how far you've come until you look back and see your progress. If there was ever a time to "trust the process," this is it.

When I formally close a coaching engagement with a client, we mark it as their start—the point where they firmly grab the baton to coach themselves and I let go. Consider this moment our close. You are ready to grow and become the leader you want to be. As you move forward with the baton, remember the words of Austrian philosopher and Holocaust survivor Viktor Frankl: "Everything can be taken from a (hu)man but one thing: the last of the human freedoms—to choose one's attitude in any given set of circumstances, to choose one's own way." When you unblock from the beliefs that hold you back, you free yourself, your team, your organization, and yes, even the world to move forward and fulfill its potential. And that, my friend, *is* leadership.

As I stand back, no longer holding the baton but cheering you from the sidelines, I leave you with the ancient words of the practice of loving-kindness meditation, as we all journey forward on the path from blocked to unblocked.

May you be happy.
May you be safe.
May you be well.
May you live (and lead) with ease.

Appendix

Coach Yourself Worksheet

Here you'll find your own Coach Yourself worksheet. Use it to coach yourself through the Blocked to Unblocked Roadmap and to answer coaching questions that will help uncover, unpack, and unblock from the primary hidden blocker that's currently holding you back. Reflect and revise as often as you need, because this can very much be an iterative process. If you get stuck, go back to the hidden blocker chapter that most resonated with you and see if it helps you move forward. Discussing with a trusted colleague or mentor can also help. (A downloadable version of this worksheet can be found at https://hbr.org /book-resources.)

An example of a completed worksheet for Alex from chapter 3 also follows. Use it as inspiration to complete your own process, but remember, everyone's worksheet will look different because everyone's hidden blockers affect them and their leadership uniquely.

Your hidden blocker: _____	
Coach Yourself questions:	
Stage 1: Uncover your hidden blocker	**Step 1: Realize you're blocked. What are signs that you're blocked from your leadership potential?** • *Where in your work are you not seeing the results you desire? What specific areas feel stuck or unproductive?* • *Where do you notice a gap between your intentions and the actual impact you're making? How might others be experiencing your actions differently from how you intend?* • *Who could offer you valuable feedback to help identify blind spots or performance gaps? What specific questions can you ask to gain clearer insights?*
	Step 2: Name your hidden blocker. What is the limiting belief that's blocking you from achieving the impact you want? • *What are the different ways your hidden blocker can be named?* • *What phrase do you often think to yourself as you're running into challenges at work?* • *What is your internal dialogue telling you?*
Stage 2: Unpack your hidden blocker	**Step 3: Accept your hidden blocker. What gets in the way of you fully owning the impact of your limiting belief?** • *When you reflect on the challenge you're facing, what role are you playing in creating or sustaining it? How might you be contributing to the issue?* • *How do you tend to justify or defend your behavior in this situation? What explanations do you use to support your actions or beliefs?* • *What do you gain or lose by holding on to this belief? How is it serving you, and in what ways might it be holding you back?*

	Step 4: Deconstruct your hidden blocker. What experiences or influences have shaped this belief? • Who or what situations have reinforced this belief over time? How did these people or experiences contribute to solidifying it? • In what ways has this hidden blocker been helpful or protective for you in the past? What purpose has it served? • How does this belief serve you in your current context? In what ways might it be outdated or limiting?
Stage 3: Unblock from your hidden blocker	**Step 5: Reframe your blocker. What belief would better support the leadership impact you aspire to have?** • What specific impact do you want to have as a leader? How would you like others to experience your leadership? • What new belief could you adopt that would enable you to achieve this desired impact? How might this belief shift your approach and influence?
	Step 6: Take action. What actions will you take to move from feeling blocked to feeling unblocked? • What specific steps can you take that are aligned with your new supportive belief? How can you bring this belief to life through action? • What can you start doing, and what can you stop doing, to reinforce and stay aligned with this new belief? How will these adjustments support your growth?

Alex's hidden blocker: *I need to be involved.*	
Stage 1: Uncover your hidden blocker	**Step 1: Realize you're blocked. What are signs that you're blocked from your leadership potential?** • *I don't have time to be more strategic in my role because I get pulled into the weeds.* • *I don't have the bandwidth to cultivate the external relationships that I need to.* • *My schedule is jam-packed with meetings, and I often find myself double-booked.* • *I am copied on numerous emails and find my inbox overwhelming.* • *My recent 360-degree feedback stated that I'm a "micromanager."*
	Step 2: Name your hidden blocker. What is the limiting belief that's blocking you from achieving the impact you want? • *I have to be involved in the details or something will go wrong.*
Stage 2: Unpack your hidden blocker	**Step 3: Accept your hidden blocker. What gets in the way of you fully owning the impact of your limiting belief?** • *I didn't ask for this; my team and peers want me to be involved.* • *They're not capable of doing it, so I have to.* • *This is how I operate, and it hasn't failed me yet.* • *I need to know what's going on with everything in case my boss or another stakeholder asks me.* • *I need to be involved to make sure everything gets done.*
	Step 4: Deconstruct your hidden blocker. What experiences or influences have shaped this belief? • *I've always made sure to have all my bases covered and it's helped me get where I am. It's what enabled me to be a great athlete—not just knowing my position but also those of my teammates.* • *A boss once chewed me out for not checking on someone else's work. Even though it was my colleague's mistake, I promised myself I'd never put myself in that position again.*
Stage 3: Unblock from your hidden blocker	**Step 5: Reframe your blocker. What belief would better support the leadership impact you aspire to have?** • *I need to mainly be involved where I add the most value.*
	Step 6: Take action. What actions will you take to move from feeling blocked to feeling unblocked? • *Prioritize the top involvement areas specific to my role, where only I can add value and make sure my calendar reflects them.* • *Determine which meetings need my involvement and schedule accordingly.* • *Delegate other tasks to appropriate team members.*

Notes

Chapter 1

1. Carol S. Dweck, *Mindset: The New Psychology of Success* (New York: Random House, 2006), ix, 6.

2. Albert Bandura, "Cultivate Self-Efficacy for Personal and Organizational Effectiveness," in *Handbook of Principles of Organizational Behavior*, 2nd ed., ed. E. A. Locke (New York: Wiley, 2009), 179–200.

3. Alia J. Crum and Ellen J. Langer, "Mind-Set Matters: Exercise and the Placebo Effect," *Psychological Science* 18, no. 2 (2007): 165–71, doi: 10.1111/j.1467-9280.2007.01867.x.

4. Alia Crum, "The Science of How Mindset Transforms the Human Experience," YouTube video, February 21, 2018, https://www.youtube.com/watch?v=vTDYtwqKBI8.

5. Shirzad Chamine, *Positive Intelligence: Why Only 20% of Teams and Individuals Achieve Their True Potential and HOW YOU CAN ACHIEVE YOURS* (Austin, TX: Greenleaf Book Group Press, 2012).

6. Jana Siebert and Johannes U. Siebert, "Effective Mitigation of the Belief Perseverance Bias after the Retraction of Misinformation: Awareness Training and Counter-Speech," *PLoS One* 18, no. 3 (March 8, 2023), doi: 10.1371/journal.pone.0282202.

7. Linda Graham, *Bouncing Back: Rewiring Your Brain for Maximum Resilience and Well-Being* (Novato, CA: New World Library, 2013).

8. Justin James Kennedy, "Becoming a Natural Leader Through Brain Adaptability," *Psychology Today*, August 2, 2023, https://www.psychologytoday.com/us/blog/brain-reboot/202308/becoming-a-natural-leader-through-brain-adaptability.

Chapter 2

1. Tasha Eurich, "What Self-Awareness Really Is (and How to Cultivate It)," hbr.org, January 4, 2018, https://hbr.org/2018/01/what-self-awareness-really-is-and-how-to-cultivate-it.

2. Matthew D. Lieberman et al., "Putting Feelings into Words," *Psychological Science* 18, no. 5 (2007): 421–28, https://doi.org/10.1111/j.1467-9280.2007.01916.x.

3. Richard E. Boyatzis, Annie McKee, and Daniel Goleman, *Primal Leadership: Unleashing the Power of Emotional Intelligence* (Boston: Harvard Business Review Press, 2013), 171–72, 204–205.

4. Klodiana Lanaj, Trevor A. Foulk, and Remy E. Jennings, "Improving the Lives of Leaders: The Beneficial Effects of Positive Leader Self-Reflection," *Journal of Management* 49, no. 8 (2023): 2595–628, https://doi.org/10.1177 /01492063221110205.

5. Francesca Gino and Bradley Staats, "The Remedy for Unproductive Busyness," hbr.org, April 24, 2015, https://hbr.org/2015/04/the-remedy-for -unproductive-busyness.

6. James Bigley II, "The Truth behind a Self-Fulfilling Prophecy," *Cleveland Clinic* (blog), January 6, 2023, https://health.clevelandclinic.org/self-fulfilling -prophecy/.

Chapter 3

1. Frances Bridges, "The 3 Steps of Essentialism: How to Achieve More by Doing Less, According to Author Greg McKeown," *Forbes*, November 9, 2018, https://www.forbes.com/sites/francesbridges/2018/11/29/the-3-steps-of -essentialism-achieving-more-by-doing-less-according-to-greg-mckeown/?sh =300bb1b51b9b.

2. Archy O. de Berker et al., "Computations of Uncertainty Mediate Acute Stress Responses in Humans," *Nature Communications* 7, no. 10996 (2016), https://doi.org/10.1038/ncomms10996.

Chapter 4

1. Sabine Sonnentag, Bonnie Hayden Cheng, and Stacey L. Parker, "Recovery from Work: Advancing the Field toward the Future," *Annual Review of Organizational Psychology and Organizational Behavior* 9, no. 1 (January 21, 2022): 33–60, https://doi.org/10.1146/annurev-orgpsych-012420-091355.

2. Susie Mesure, "Wellbeing Expert Oliver Burkeman Told Me to Stare at the Robine Painting for Three Hours to Improve My Patience," *Art History News*, August 26, 2021, https://www.arthistorynews.com/articles/6636_Stare_at_the _Robine_Painting_for_Three_Hours_to_Improve_Patience.

3. Christine Riggeri, "Research Shows Hustle Culture Does More Harm Than Good," *Leaders*, May 16, 2023, https://leaders.com/articles/company-culture /hustle-culture/.

4. Brad Waters, "Zen and the Art of the Hedonic Treadmill," *Psychology Today*, December 29, 2020, https://www.psychologytoday.com/us/blog/design -your-path/202012/zen-and-the-art-the-hedonic-treadmill.

5. Jonathan Malesic, "Taming the Demon: How Desert Monks Put Work in Its Place," *Commonweal*, February 2, 2019, https://www.commonwealmagazine .org/taming-demon.

Chapter 5

1. Donald Sull et al., "Why Every Leader Needs to Worry About Toxic Culture," *MIT Sloan Management Review*, March 16, 2022, https://sloanreview .mit.edu/article/why-every-leader-needs-to-worry-about-toxic-culture.

2. Emma Seppälä and Nicole K. McNichols, "The Power of Healthy Relationships at Work," hbr.org, June 21, 2022, https://hbr.org/2022/06/the-power-of -healthy-relationships-at-work.

3. In the event that any recording is involved or if I participate in a meeting as an observer, I obtain the permission of all participants beforehand.

4. Steven D'Souza and Diana Renner, "New Managers Don't Have to Have All the Answers," hbr.org, September 30, 2015, https://hbr.org./2015/09/new -managers-Philipt-have-to-have-all-the-answers.

Chapter 6

1. Etienne Benson, "The Many Faces of Perfectionism," American Psychological Association, November 2003, https://www.apa.org/monitor/nov03/ manyfaces.

2. Lisa Capretto, "Overcoming Perfectionism: Brené Brown Talks Perfection and Authenticity with Oprah," *HuffPost*, June 29, 2013, https://www.huffpost .com/entry/brene-brown-daring-greatly-perfectionism-oprah_n_3468501.

3. Tom Curran, interview with Adam Grant, *WorkLife with Adam Grant*, podcast audio, May 3, 2022, https://www.ted.com/podcasts/worklife/breaking -up-with-perfectionism-transcript.

4. Kevin Dickinson, "How to Find Success with the 4 Conditions of 'Intelligent Failure,'" Big Think, December 11, 2023, https://bigthink.com/the-learning -curve/ntelligent-failure/.

Chapter 7

1. Leon F. Seltzer, "If I Can Do It, You Can Do It. Oh Really?," *Psychology Today*, January 5, 2021, https://www.psychologytoday.com/us/blog/evolution-the -self/202101/if-i-can-do-it-you-can-do-it-oh-really.

2. Dan Pilat and Sekoul Krastev, "Why Do We Believe We Have an Objective Understanding of the World? Naive Realism, Explained," The Decision Lab, https://thedecisionlab.com/biases/naive-realism, accessed May 17, 2024.

3. Seltzer, "If I Can Do It, You Can Do It. Oh Really?"

4. Beata Souders, "The Science of Improving Motivation at Work," Positive Psychology, January 14, 2021, https://positivepsychology.com/improving -motivation-at-work/.

5. The Platinum Rule was popularized in the eponymous book by Drs. Tony Alessandra and Michael J. O'Connor, but was originally coined in a 1979 essay called "Overcoming the Golden Rule: Sympathy and Empathy" by sociologist

Milton J. Bennett. In Bennett's version, the Platinum Rule is styled after the language of the King James Bible: "Do unto others as they themselves would have done unto them."

6. These ideas are based on a loose adaptation of the Situational Leadership Model by Drs. Paul Hersey and Alex Blanchard. For more, see https://situational.com/situational-leadership/.

Chapter 8

1. I first heard options laid out in this way by Shefali Tsabary, clinical psychologist and author.

2. Noel Burch, an employee with Gordon Training International, developed the original model in the 1970s.

3. "The Enmeshed Family System: What It Is and How to Break Free," Psych Central, May 3, 2019, https://psychcentral.com/blog/imperfect/2019/05/the-enmeshed-family-system-what-it-is-and-how-to-break-free.

4. Vanessa K. Bohns et al., "Underestimating Our Influence over Others' Unethical Behavior and Decisions," *Personality and Social Psychology Bulletin* 40, no. 3 (December 9, 2013): 348–62, https://doi.org/10.1177/0146167213511825.

5. Ahona Guha, "How (and Why) to Say No," Psych Central, June 14, 2021, https://psychcentral.com/lib/learning-to-say-no#why-its-hard.

6. "The Internal Family Systems Model Outline," IFS Institute, 2023, https://ifs-institute.com/resources/articles/internal-family-systems-model-outline.

7. I first heard this win-some/win-some idea from my friend Garry Jenkins when he taught a course on leadership at the Moritz College of Law at Ohio State University. Jenkins is now president of Bates College.

8. Prentis Hemphill, *What It Takes to Heal: How Transforming Ourselves Can Change the World* (New York: Random House, 2024), 81.

Chapter 9

1. Daniel A. Cox, Kelsey Eyre Hammond, and Jessie Wall, "Despite Professional Successes Many Women Still Experience Imposter Syndrome," Survey Center for American Life, March 15, 2023, https://www.americansurveycenter.org/women-are-achieving-greater-professional-success-yet-self-doubt-is-common/; Kevin Cokley, "It's Time to Reconceptualize What 'Impostor Syndrome' Means for People of Color," hbr.org, March 14, 2024, https://hbr.org/2024/03/its-time-to-reconceptualize-what-imposter-syndrome-means-for-people-of-color.

2. Dena M. Bravata et al., "Prevalence, Predictors, and Treatment of Impostor Syndrome: A Systematic Review," *Journal of General Internal Medicine* 35, no. 4 (2020): 1252–75, doi: 10.1007/s11606-019-05364-1.

3. Saga Pardede and Velibor Bobo Kovač, "Distinguishing the Need to Belong and Sense of Belongingness: The Relation between Need to Belong and Personal

Appraisals under Two Different Belongingness–Conditions," *European Journal of Investigation in Health, Psychology and Education* 13, no. 2 (2023): 331–44, https://doi.org/10.3390/ejihpe13020025.

4. Kevin Cokley, "Interview with Shankar Vedantam," *Hidden Brain* (podcast), May 22, 2023, https://hiddenbrain.org/podcast/the-psychology-of-self-doubt/.

5. Elisa Dermendzhiyska, "Health Warning: Social Rejection Doesn't Only Hurt—It Kills: Aeon Essays," Aeon, April 30, 2019, https://aeon.co/essays/health-warning-social-rejection-doesnt-only-hurt-it-kills.

6. Ruchika Tulshyan and Jodi-Ann Burey, "Stop Telling Women They Have Imposter Syndrome," hbr.org, February 11, 2021, https://hbr.org/2021/02/stop-telling-women-they-have-imposter-syndrome.

7. Natalie Mallal (Morad), "Part 1: How to Be an Adult—Kegan's Theory of Adult Development," *Medium*, September 28, 2017, https://medium.com/@NataliMorad/how-to-be-an-adult-kegans-theory-of-adult-development-d63f4311b553.

Chapter 10

1. Jack Zenger and Joseph Folkman, "The Trickle-Down Effect of Good (and Bad) Leadership," hbr.org, January 14, 2016, https://hbr.org/2016/01/the-trickle-down-effect-of-good-and-bad-leadership.

2. Phillip S. Thompson and Anthony C. Klotz, "Led by Curiosity and Responding with Voice: The Influence of Leader Displays of Curiosity and Leader Gender on Follower Reactions of Psychological Safety and Voice," *Organizational Behavior and Human Decision Processes* 172 (September 2022), https://doi.org/10.1016/j.obhdp.2022.104170.

3. Bob Anderson, "The Spirit of Leadership," LC White Paper Series, Leadership Circle, Draper, UT, 2021.

4. Anderson, "The Spirit of Leadership."

Index

acceptance, seeking, 193–194
accepting hidden blockers, 31–32
actions
    beliefs and, 34–35
    See also unblocking hidden blockers
active leadership, 208
active listening, 105
adaptive perfectionism, 116
advancement, lack of, 172
affect labeling, 29
American dream, 151–152
Anderson, Bob, 220, 221
Anhalt, Emily, 175
Argyris, Chris, 98
arrows parable, 223–224
assumptions about others. *See* "If I can do it, so can you" hidden blocker
assumptions about ourselves, 6–7. *See also* hidden blockers
author's experiences, 3–6
    "I can't say no" hidden blocker, 173
    "If I can do it, so can you" hidden blocker, 152–153
    "I know I'm right" hidden blocker, 96–97
    "I need it done now" hidden blocker, 75–77
    "I need to be involved" hidden blocker, 51–52
awareness of blockers, 26–28

beliefs
    actions and, 34–35
    defined, 15
    influence of, 13–16
    as interpretation of facts, 17–18
    reframing, 33–34, 217
    source of limiting beliefs, 20–23
    supportive versus limiting, 16–20
belonging. *See* "I don't belong here" hidden blocker
Blocked to Unblocked Roadmap, 25–26
    unblocking hidden blockers, 33–35
    uncovering hidden blockers, 26–30
    unpacking hidden blockers, 30–32
blockers, hidden. *See* hidden blockers
boundaries, setting, 180
breaks, importance of, 69
Brown, Brené, 125
Burkeman, Oliver, 70
burnout, 72, 74, 172

challenges, approach to, 7–8
Chamine, Shirzad, 17
CIA (context, intent, actions), 157
coaching
    therapy versus, 10–11
    unblocked leadership example, 209–218

coaching tips
  "I can't make a mistake" hidden
    blocker, 132–134
  "I can't say no" hidden blocker,
    180–182
  "I don't belong here" hidden
    blocker, 202–203
  "If I can do it, so can you" hidden
    blocker, 158–160
  "I know I'm right" hidden blocker,
    103–105
  "I need it done now" hidden
    blocker, 81–82
  "I need to be involved" hidden
    blocker, 56–58
Coach Yourself worksheet, 227–230
cognitive dissonance, 35
Cokley, Kevin, 196
comparison with others, 125
Conscious Competence Ladder,
  169–170
conscious competence model, 169
costs
  "I can't make a mistake" hidden
    blocker, 122–123
  "I can't say no" hidden blocker,
    172
  "I don't belong here" hidden
    blocker, 194–195
  "If I can do it, so can you" hidden
    blocker, 148–149
  "I know I'm right" hidden blocker, 95
  "I need it done now" hidden
    blocker, 72–73
  "I need to be involved" hidden
    blocker, 50
Crum, Alia, 15–16
curiosity, 212–213
Curran, Thomas, 125–126

decision checklist, 128
decision-making, 112–114, 120–122
deconstructing hidden blockers, 32

defensiveness, 214
deficit thinking, 125
doing nothing, 70–71
double-loop learning, 98–99
D'Souza, Steven, 99
Dweck, Carol, 13–14

Edmondson, Amy, 132
Einstein, Albert, 220
excellence, striving for, 127
exhaustion, 72, 172
exploitation, 172
external validation, 196–198

facts, interpretation of, 17–18
failure
  handling, 98, 116, 132
  risk of, 149
Father Simeon, 79
fears. See "I can't say no" hidden
  blocker
fixed mindset, 14
Flett, Gordon, 117
focus, shifting, 8
Four Thousand Weeks: Time
  Management for Mortals
  (Burkeman), 70
Frankl, Viktor, 226

golden rule, 155
Goldsmith, Marshall, 159
grace, 225
Graham, Linda, 19
Grant, Adam, 125
growth mindset, 14
guiding, leadership as, 100–101, 208

hedonic adaptation, 76
Hemphill, Prentis, 180
Hewitt, Paul, 117

hidden blockers
    accepting, 31–32
    Blocked to Unblocked Roadmap,
        25–26
    deconstructing, 32
    defined, 7
    examples of, 9
    "I can't make a mistake,"
        107–134
    "I can't say no," 161–182
    "I don't belong here," 183–203
    "If I can do it, so can you,"
        135–160
    "I know I'm right," 83–105
    "I need it done now," 59–82
    "I need to be involved," 39–58
    list of, 23–24
    naming, 29–30, 212–213
    signs of, 27
    unblocking, 33–35
    uncovering, 26–30
    unpacking, 30–32
    See also limiting beliefs
hustle culture, 74

"I can't make a mistake" hidden
        blocker, 107–134
    coaching tips, 132–134
    costs of, 122–123
    introductory story, 107–109
    signs of, 115
    source of, 122–126
    unblocking, 126–132
    uncovering, 109–115
    unpacking, 116–126
"I can't say no" hidden blocker,
        161–182
    coaching tips, 180–182
    costs of, 172
    introductory story, 161–163
    signs of, 166
    source of, 173–175
    unblocking, 176–180

    uncovering, 163–167
    unpacking, 167–175
"I don't belong here" hidden blocker,
        183–203
    coaching tips, 202–203
    costs of, 194–195
    introductory story, 183–184
    signs of, 186
    source of, 195–199
    unblocking, 199–202
    uncovering, 184–187
    unpacking, 187–199
"If I can do it, so can you" hidden
        blocker, 135–160
    coaching tips, 158–160
    costs of, 148–149
    introductory story, 135–138
    signs of, 143
    source of, 150–154
    unblocking, 154–158
    uncovering, 138–144
    unpacking, 144–154
"I know I'm right" hidden blocker,
        83–105
    coaching tips, 103–105
    costs of, 95
    introductory story, 83–85
    signs of, 90
    source of, 95–99
    unblocking, 99–103
    uncovering, 85–91
    unpacking, 91–99
impostor syndrome, 187, 197
inauthenticity, 194
"I need it done now" hidden blocker,
        59–82
    coaching tips, 81–82
    costs of, 72–73
    introductory story, 59–61
    signs of, 66–67
    source of, 74–77
    unblocking, 77–81
    uncovering, 61–67
    unpacking, 67–77

"I need to be involved" hidden blocker, 39–58
  coaching tips, 56–58
  costs of, 50
  introductory story, 39–41
  signs of, 44
  source of, 49–53
  unblocking, 53–56
  uncovering, 42–44
  unpacking, 44–53
insecurity, 151
internal family systems model, 176
interpretation of facts, beliefs as, 17–18
intimacy, 215

jar exercise, 118–120

Kegan, Robert, 198
Kennedy, Justin James, 19
knowledge. *See* "I know I'm right" hidden blocker

leadership, unblocked. *See* unblocked leadership
learned helplessness, 95
learning, single-loop and double-loop, 98–99
limiting beliefs
  defined, 16
  at organizational level, 220
  protective nature of, 20–22
  source of, 20–23
  supportive beliefs versus, 16–20
  See also hidden blockers

maladaptive perfectionism, 116–117
Malesic, Jonathan, 79
Maslow, Abraham, 21, 195
McKeown, Greg, 42
meditation, 70

micromanagement. *See* "I need to be involved" hidden blocker
mindset, 13–14, 221. *See also* beliefs
missed opportunities, 194
mistakes. *See* "I can't make a mistake" hidden blocker
motivation. *See* "If I can do it, so can you" hidden blocker

naive realism, 150–151
naming hidden blockers, 29–30, 212–213
needs, Maslow's hierarchy of, 21, 195
neuroplasticity, 19

organizational level of unblocked leadership, 219–222
other-oriented perfectionism, 117, 148, 151

pain, response to, 6
parable of the second arrow, 223–224
passive leadership, 208
patience, 225
peer-coaching, 225
peloton, 84
perfectionism, 116–117, 122–126, 148, 151, 195
personal relationships, harm to, 73
platinum rule, 155
pleasing people. *See* "I can't say no" hidden blocker
Positive Intelligence (Chamine), 17
prioritization. *See* "I need it done now" hidden blocker; "I need to be involved" hidden blocker
problem-solving, 98
procrastination, 122
productivity. *See* "I need it done now" hidden blocker

protective nature of limiting beliefs,
    20–22
psychological safety, 148, 195

quiet quitting, 148

racialized impostor phenomenon,
    187
reframing beliefs, 33–34, 217
rejection, fear of, 193, 196
relationship building, 194
Renner, Diana, 99
resentment, 172
response to pain, 6
risk aversion, 195
risk intolerance, 122
risk of failure, 149
risk of unethical behavior, 149
Roberts, Jennifer, 70
Roosevelt, Theodore, 125

safety, need for, 50–53
saying no. *See* "I can't say no" hidden
    blocker
Schwartz, Richard, 176
second arrow parable, 223–224
self-awareness, 26–28, 87
self-efficacy, 14
self-esteem, 151
self-oriented perfectionism, 117
self-reflection, 30, 98
self-talk, 20
Seltzer, Leon, 150
signs of hidden blockers, 27
    "I can't make a mistake" hidden
        blocker, 115
    "I can't say no" hidden blocker,
        166
    "I don't belong here" hidden
        blocker, 186
    "If I can do it, so can you" hidden
        blocker, 143

"I know I'm right" hidden blocker, 90
"I need it done now" hidden
    blocker, 66–67
"I need to be involved" hidden
    blocker, 44
single-loop learning, 98
social awareness, 87
socially prescribed perfectionists,
    117
societal conditioning, 151–152
strategic leadership. *See* "I need to be
    involved" hidden blocker
subject-matter expertise. *See* "I know
    I'm right" hidden blocker
supportive beliefs, 16–20
systemic bias, 197

"Teaching Smart People How to
    Learn" (Argyris), 98
teams
    alienation and low morale, 95
    division in, 73
therapy, coaching versus, 10–11
toxic productivity, 75

unblocked leadership
    coaching example, 209–218
    at organizational level,
        219–222
    passive versus active, 208
unblocking hidden blockers,
    33–35
    coaching example, 216–218
    "I can't make a mistake,"
        126–132
    "I can't say no," 176–180
    "I don't belong here," 199–202
    "If I can do it, so can you,"
        154–158
    "I know I'm right," 99–103
    "I need it done now," 77–81
    "I need to be involved,"
        53–56

uncovering hidden blockers,
    26–30
  coaching example, 210–211
  "I can't make a mistake," 109–115
  "I can't say no," 163–167
  "I don't belong here," 184–187
  "If I can do it, so can you," 138–144
  "I know I'm right," 85–91
  "I need it done now," 61–67
  "I need to be involved," 42–44
unethical behavior, risk of, 149
unpacking hidden blockers, 30–32
  coaching example, 212–216
  "I can't make a mistake," 116–126

"I can't say no," 167–175
"I don't belong here," 187–199
"If I can do it, so can you," 144–154
"I know I'm right," 91–99
"I need it done now," 67–77
"I need to be involved," 44–53

validation, 193, 196–198
visualization, 101
vulnerability, 215

worst-case scenario exercise, 129–131

Acknowledgments

This book could not have come to life without my village. A deep bow to everyone who touched it—sometimes without even knowing it.

To my agent, Giles Anderson—thank you for fielding my endless questions, seeing the possibility, and being an all-around stand-up human. I'm delighted to have had the chance to do this with you again.

To Catherine Knepper—thank you for your wisdom, warmth, and grounded presence. You started as my writing coach and became a confidante, reminding me that kindred spirits still exist.

To the early readers of *Leadership Unblocked*—Adam Grant, Michael Bungay Stanier, Dorie Clark, Frances Frei, Michelle Riley-Brown, Tom Monahan, and Magdalena Nowicka Mook. Thank you for answering my call. I'm deeply humbled by your support and generosity of time.

To the Harvard Business Review Press team—thank you for always making me feel like family. I can't imagine a better home for this book. Courtney Cashman, editor extraordinaire, thank you for believing in this project and for knowing exactly when to encourage, nudge, and when to push back. You are a master of your craft. Thank you to Julie Devoll, Alexandra Kephart, Emma Waldman, Stephani Finks, Jennifer Waring, and everyone else involved in making this book come to life. I appreciate all of you. Amy Bernstein, thank you for your steady kindness and openness. Amy Gallo, thank you for being both a brilliant colleague and a dear friend. Your ongoing support and the fact that you always text me back means more than I can say.

To Nina Nocciolino and Barbara Henricks—I knew you were my people from that first call. Thank you for bringing your magic to the launch of this book.

To the *Coaching Real Leaders* podcast community—Mary Dooe, you are the best producer I could ask for. You get me, and I'm so grateful. Much appreciation to Maureen Hoch, Ian Fox, and Hannah Bates for all the ways you've supported the show. To my awesome CRL community members—thank you for the discussions, the sharing, the questions, and for graciously tolerating my rants and rambles. I've learned so much from you! To CRL listeners—you make it all worth it.

To the Paravis team—thank you for your steadfastness. You are a powerhouse and I'm proud of the work we do together to help leaders grow. A very special shout-out to my rock, Emily Sopha. I truly don't know what I'd do without you. You're stuck with me.

To all my executive coaching clients—thank you for trusting me with your evolutions. It's an honor I never take lightly. While I can't name you (those NDAs are tight!), you know who you are, and I see you. Without you, this book wouldn't exist. And to the organizational sponsors who bring me and my team in—thank you for your trust and partnership, especially Mara Dell, Meghan Young, and Ann Anastasia.

To the guides who have helped me see more clearly—especially Santa Molina-Marshall, Dené Logan, and Shefali Tsabary, whose coaching I've been fortunate to experience firsthand—and to those whose wisdom I've absorbed from afar: Glennon Doyle, Esther Perel, Pema Chödrön, Thich Nhat Hanh, Michael Singer, Richard Schwartz, Robert Kegan, Gabor Maté, MD, and Melody Beattie. Your insights live in these pages and have deeply influenced my work. And to the many others whose words or work have shaped me as a coach and human in ways I may not even fully recognize—thank you.

To Papa, Marie-Jude, Nancy, and Genevieve—thank you for making space for this last star in our family constellation to shine in her own way. And Maman—I miss you every day. While I'm still learning how to walk in this world without you here, your spirit runs deep within me. Je t'embrasse.

To my beautiful sister-friends—I'm immensely blessed to have you in my life. You are phenomenal women who hold me down, lift me up, make me laugh, keep it real, and let me be fully myself. I'm especially grateful for my Oasis Crew and BGM Tread Tribe for keeping me moving in so many ways. I especially have endless gratitude for Josephine, Cami, Kaya, Mannone, Natalie, Shereen, Pam, Amber, Kim, Adrienne, Jaqee, and my ultimate ride or die, Samantha, for all the ways you enthusiastically celebrate and encourage me—I give you your flowers. Thank you for always being my soft landings.

To Arden—thank you for being the mirror that helped me find my way back to my Self. Thank you for choosing to walk this life with me. Thank you for seeing me. I will always meet you in the garden.

To Noah and Gabi—thank you for being exactly who you are and for choosing me to be your mommy. Thank you for teaching me to laugh and find joy, even when the world says otherwise. Thank you for gifting me the experience of unconditional love that surpasses all understanding. My one sacred job as your mom has been to love you well, and I will never ever give that up. Love you more!

About the Author

For over two decades, Muriel Maignan Wilkins has been a trusted adviser and executive coach to high-performing C-suite and senior executives, helping them navigate their most complex challenges with clarity and confidence. As founder and CEO of Paravis Partners, a leadership advisory firm, she and her team partner with leaders to increase their impact and achieve meaningful results.

Clients have called Wilkins a "CEO whisperer," a "vault," and, memorably, "my personal Olivia Pope—but without all the drama." Her ability to combine strategic insight with deep emotional intelligence has made her a sought-after coach for those leading at the highest levels.

Wilkins is the host of the award-winning HBR podcast *Coaching Real Leaders* and coauthor of *Own the Room: Discover Your Signature Voice to Master Your Leadership Presence*. She is also a contributor to the *HBR Guide to Coaching Employees* and a frequent speaker on how leaders can get unstuck and overcome internal and external roadblocks.

Before founding Paravis, Wilkins held leadership roles in management consulting, strategy, and marketing. She earned her MBA from Harvard Business School and her BSBA and leadership coaching certificate from Georgetown University.

Raised in North Africa, Europe, and the Caribbean, Wilkins brings a global perspective to her work and a guiding principle that we are collectively stronger when we lead from a place of shared humanity. She now calls Washington, DC, home. A lifelong wisdom seeker, she is deeply committed to human rights and believes that how people are led has a profound impact on their lives.

Wilkins's mission is simple but powerful: to help leaders grow and evolve so they—and those around them—can lead and live with greater ease.

You can connect with Muriel Wilkins and access free resources at murielwilkins.com.